Columbia University

New York, New York

Written by Julia Green and Michelle Tompkins
Edited by Kai Dawson

Additional contributions by Omid Gohari,
Christina Koshzow, Chris Mason, Joey Rahimi,
Jon Skindzier, Luke Skurman, Tim Williams

ISBN # 1-59658-034-8
ISSN #: 1551-0285
© Copyright 2005 College Prowler
All Rights Reserved
Printed in the U.S.A.
www.collegeprowler.com

Special thanks to Babs Carryer, Andy Hannah, LaunchCyte, Tim O'Brien, Bob Sehlinger, Thomas Emerson, Andrew Skurman, Barbara Skurman, Bert Mann, Dave Lehman, Daniel Fayock, Chris Babyak,The Donald H. Jones Center for Entrepreneurship, Terry Slease, Jerry McGinnis, Bill Ecenberger, Idie McGinty, Kyle Russell, Jacque Zaremba, Larry Winderbaum, Paul Kelly, Roland Allen, Jon Reider, Team Evankovich, Julie Fenstermaker, Lauren Varacalli, Abu Noaman, Jason Putorti, Mark Exler, Daniel Steinmeyer, Jared Cohon, Gabriela Oates, Tri Ad Litho, David Koegler, Glen Meakem, and the Columbia University bounce back team.

College Prowler™
5001 Baum Blvd.
Suite 456
Pittsburgh, PA 15213

Phone: (412) 697-1390, 1(800) 290-2682
Fax: (412) 697-1396, 1(800) 772-4972
E-mail: info@collegeprowler.com
Website: www.collegeprowler.com

Welcome to College Prowler™

During the writing of College Prowler's guidebooks, we felt it was critical that our content was unbiased and unaffiliated with any college or university. We think it's important that our readers get honest information and a realistic impression of the student opinions on any campus — that's why if any aspect of a particular school is terrible, we (unlike a campus brochure) intend to publish it. While we do keep an eye out for the occasional extremist — the cheerleader or the cynic — we take pride in letting the students tell it like it is. We strive to create a book that's as representative as possible of each particular campus. Our books cover both the good and the bad, and whether the survey responses point to recurring trends or a variation in opinion, these sentiments are directly and proportionally expressed through our guides.

College Prowler guidebooks are in the hands of students throughout the entire process of their creation. Because you can't make student-written guides without the students, we have students at each campus who help write, randomly survey their peers, edit, layout, and perform accuracy checks on every book that we publish. From the very beginning, student writers gather the most up-to-date stats, facts, and inside information on their colleges. They fill each section with student quotes and summarize the findings in editorial reviews. In addition, each school receives a collection of letter grades (A through F) that reflect student opinion and help to represent contentment, prominence, or satisfaction for each of our 20 specific categories. Just as in grade school, the higher the mark the more content, more prominent, or more satisfied the students are with the particular category.

Once a book is written, additional students serve as editors and check for accuracy even more extensively. Our bounce-back team — a group of randomly selected students who have no involvement with the project — are asked to read over the material in order to help ensure that the book accurately expresses every aspect of the university and its students. This same process is applied to the 200-plus schools College Prowler currently covers. Each book is the result of endless student contributions, hundreds of pages of research and writing, and countless hours of hard work. All of this has led to the creation of a student information network that stretches across the nation to every school that we cover. It's no easy accomplishment, but it's the reason that our guides are such a great resource.

When reading our books and looking at our grades, keep in mind that every college is different and that the students who make up each school are not uniform — as a result, it is important to assess schools on a case-by-case basis. Because it's impossible to summarize an entire school with a single number or description, each book provides a dialogue, not a decision, that's made up of 20 different topics and hundreds of student quotes. In the end, we hope that this guide will serve as a valuable tool in your college selection process. Enjoy!

OMID GOHARI ◯ CHRISTINA KOSHZOW ◯ CHRIS MASON ◯ JOEY RAHIMI ◯ LUKE SKURMAN ◯
The College Prowler™ Team

Table of Contents

Introduction from the Author

"You're shooting too low," said my teacher as I told her my selection of colleges. Because I am the type of student known more for contributions outside the classroom than pure scholastic ability, gaining admittance to my first-choice college seemed like a long shot. I applied to Columbia, the school of my dreams, to appease others and just to see if I could possibly make this dream a reality. I waited for my acceptance or rejection letter, which never came. I called the school to find out what was happening, but my application had been shuttled to another department and no information was forthcoming. Maybe they were just trying to spare my feelings and possibly avoid a teary scene. Either way I took this as a bad sign, and immediately began plans for attending my back-up school. I went to lunch with my mother and sadly told her the news. When we returned home, I found a note written in three different colors of ink taped to the front door. The note read, "Michelle, check the answering machine. Have a pen ready. Call me when you are through. Love, Dad." On the machine was a frantic message from my erstwhile academic counselor begging me to call Columbia. It turns out that my information had been misplaced and they wanted to advise me of my acceptance so I could begin the necessary paperwork. I knew then that nothing could exceed the excitement of getting accepted to Columbia. I was wrong. The thrill never ended. My relationship with Columbia started slowly, but it turned out to be more than I ever hoped it would be: fascinating courses, eclectic people, and a reputation for excellence that dates back to 1754, not to mention having the whole city of New York as an extra appendage for self-discovery. Columbia University is a place unlike any other.

Columbia University, located in the heart of New York City provides students with both a prestigious Ivy League education and all of the diversions present in a metropolis. The University attracts the best of the best from every corner of the world and the undergraduate colleges (Columbia College, The Fu Foundation for Engineering and Applied Sciences, the School of General Studies and Barnard College) are geared to serve the wide range of personalities present here. Columbia College is the school for recent high school graduates who intend to earn a B.A. or B.S. degree. The Fu Foundation is for students who plan on pursuing careers in engineering and applied sciences. The School of General Studies serves non-traditional students, (average age 28) who have chosen to return to school after an absence. Barnard is the women's college affiliated with the university. In the following pages, you will learn from people in the know—students from three colleges under the Columbia University umbrella. I hope you find this information helpful and adding to a unique experience at a great institution, in a wonderful town.

Michelle L. Tompkins
School of General Studies

By the Numbers

General Information

Columbia University
3000 Broadway
New York, New York 10027

Control:
Private

Academic Calendar:
Semester

Religious Affiliation:
None

Founded:
1754

Website:
http://www.columbia.edu

Main Phone:
(212) 854-1754

Admissions Phone:
(212) 854-1754

Student Body

**Full-Time
Undergraduates:**
6,248

**Part-Time
Undergraduates:**
886

**Total Male
Undergraduates:**
3,749

**Total Female
Undergraduates:**
3,385

Male to Female Ratio:
53% to 47%

Admissions

Overall Acceptance Rate:
11%

Early Decision Acceptance Rate:
26%

Regular Acceptance Rate:
9%

Total Applicants:
14,648

Total Acceptances:
1,643

Freshman Enrollment:
1,011

Yield (percentage of admitted students who actually enroll):
61.5%

Early Decision Available?
Yes

Early Action Available?
No

Total Early Decision Applicants:
2389

Total Early Decision Acceptances:
624

Early Decision One Deadline:
November 1

Early Decision One Notification:
December 15

Regular Decision Deadline:
January 2

Regular Decision Notification:
April 1

Must Reply-By Date:
May 1

Common Application Accepted?
No

Admissions Phone:
(212) 854-1754

Admissions E-mail:
Ugrad-admiss@columbia.edu

Admissions Website:
www.columbia.edu/cu/admissions

SAT I or ACT Required?
SAT required.

First-Year Students Submitting SAT Scores:
100%

SAT I Range (25th – 75th Percentile):
1310 – 1510

SAT I Verbal Range (25th – 75th Percentile):
650 – 760

SAT I Math Range (25th – 75th Percentile):
660 – 750

SAT II Requirements:
For Columbia College, The writing test and any other two. For The Fu Foundation School of Engineering and Applied Sciences, The Writing test; any mathematics test; and either Physics or Chemistry.

→

→

Retention Rate:
98%

**Top 10% of
High School Class:**
81%

Application Fee:
$65

**Applicants Placed
on Waiting List:**
1,706

**Applicants Accepting
a Place on Waiting List:**
1,143

**Students Enrolled
from Waiting List:**
64

**Transfer
Applications Received:**
1,037

**Transfer Applicants
Offered Admission:**
88

Transfer Applicants Enrolled:
61

**Transfer Applicant
Acceptance Rate:**
8%

Financial Information

Tuition:
$31,472

Room and Board:
$9,066

Books and Supplies:
$2,060

**Average Need-Based
Financial Aid Package
(including loans, work-study,
grants, and other sources):**
$28,684

**Students Who Applied For
Financial Aid:**
49%

**Students Who Applied For
Financial Aid and Received It:**
42%

Financial Aid Forms Deadline
February 10

Financial Aid Phone:
(212) 854-3711

Financial Aid E-mail:
ugrad-finaid@columbia.edu

Financial Aid Website:
www.studentaffairs.columbia.
edu/finaid

Academics

The Lowdown On...
Academics

Degrees Awarded:
Certificate
Bachelor's
Post-bachelor's certificate
Master's
First professional
First professional certificate
Doctorate

Full-Time Faculty:
1,467

Faculty with Terminal Degree:
100%

Student-to-Faculty Ratio:
7:1

Graduation Rate:
Four Year: 84%
Five Year: 90%
Six Year: 92%

→

Undergraduate Schools:

- Columbia College
- The Fu Foundation School for Engineering and Applied Sciences
- The School of General Studies

Most popular majors:

28% Social Sciences

14% English Language and Literature/letters

12% History

8% Visual and Performing Arts

6% Multi/Interdisciplinary Studies

Special Degree Options
Five-year combined B.A./B.S.

AP Test Score Requirements
Placement with scores of 4 or 5.

Average Course Load
Students can take anywhere from 12 to 22 points a term, which translates to about four to seven classes, depending on how many credits a class is worth (the system is slightly convoluted at CU). Most kids take five classes a semester, but both four and six are acceptable and doable.

Did You Know?

Bring your flippers

Columbia University requires all of its undergraduates to pass a swim test in order to graduate? The test consists of swimming three lengths of the pool without stopping and it is the bane of all seniors trying to fulfill every last requirement.

Sample Academic Clubs

- Astrophysics Club
- Maison Française
- Society of Engineers

Best Places to Study

- The stacks in Butler Library
- A corner table at the Hungarian Pastry Shop
- A comfy chair in Lerner Hall.

Students Speak Out On...
Academics

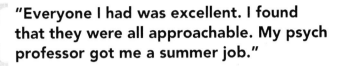

"Everyone I had was excellent. I found that they were all approachable. My psych professor got me a summer job."

Q "Use your own discretion. One student's **heartless wench** is another's brilliant educator."

Q "The good things about most of Columbia's TAs are that **they are easily accessible** to their students and they will try to work with students who are having problems in class. The bad news is that they are notoriously hard graders who are difficult to please and tend to be petty."

Q "There is a core curriculum that will take up about two years of your studies. Now, although the classes are helpful, if you aren't so sure what you want to do with your life the core could also hurt you because it prevents you from being able to try out a lot of different things with your credits. No matter what you think, **don't take more than 19 credits in one semester.** It is not worth it; trust me."

Q "A great website is http://www.columbia.edu/~msd39 (CULPA website). You have to have the professor's name, but it will give you a review and can be really helpful in picking classes. **Be sure not to base all of your decisions on it** because sometimes, you may totally disagree. But if ten people say that if they had a choice between lighting their hair on fire or taking some guy's class and they pick the fire, I'd say steer clear if you can."

Q "I'd say the math/science intro courses are a crapshoot and **will probably suck** regardless of whether or not your professor is competent."

Q "The **teachers are excellent** but you have to make sure by doing research before taking a class. There are some teachers that are definitely not worth wasting your money on. Also, there are many brilliant graduate students who have taught the best classes that I have ever had. However, be wary of the graduate students who are tough graders, arrogant and frankly a waste of your tuition. Why do you want to come to Columbia in order to take a class with a graduate student who although may have excellent grades, has very little experience teaching?"

Q "**Adjuncts are swell.** The prestigious ones are a bunch of windbags held afloat by their egos alone."

Q "Intense. At Columbia, **the teachers are uniquely committed** to shaping the minds of their students."

Q "All of my teachers at Columbia have been **truly excellent.** However, this past semester, I had an amazing, fascinating, mesmerizing teacher who taught me the philosophy of aesthetics. I also had her for another class, and believe me when I say that this woman made me want to major in philosophy. All of my instructors have been real professors, with the exception of my teacher for a mandatory freshman writing class; that one was taught by a great teaching assistant (TA)."

Q "Teachers are excellent. Even though you are placed in a big class, **you have to make time to get to know the teacher** so that you can have a good semester."

Q "Most of my experiences with teachers have been great. **Columbia has a lot of grad students and TAs, but you would never know it.** They are brilliant and young and entertaining. Most of the time, all of my teachers have been accessible and approachable."

Q "Intelligent, provocative and **well-connected** in their respective fields."

Q "There are **some good and some bad,** but as a warning, there's a wide range of teaching skills within the core itself. Some are awesome professors, and some very mediocre ones. My freshman year, I had the ideal professor, the kind you dream of. He took us out for pastries and coffee. We went on a search for beauty in New York City, took walks in Central Park, and visited the Met and a modern gallery."

Q "I guess the teachers are like anywhere else. You have those who are **so amazing** that you can't believe you're in their class, and you'll have those that you won't be able to believe Columbia hired. That's college life, but there is a cool web page that you can access through the Columbia website called 'CULPA' that allows you to read students opinions on teachers. It helped me a lot second semester."

Q "The teachers can really vary. I've had some excellent teachers but **plenty of mediocre ones as well.** In some math and science-type areas, there are lots of unintelligible, foreign professors. Overall, I'd say the professors are pretty good and more or less what you'd expect from a big research university. Most are pretty accessible. However, in some popular majors, the classes can be really large, so there's little interaction with them."

Q "The professors here are generally great. **They are very knowledgeable.** They all have high degrees and come from top institutions. They are some, however, that can be really smart but can't teach. But, overall, professors are great. Take advantage of them! They're always willing to meet up with students outside of class. They're really interesting! Their availability is pretty good, depending on the professors. Most of them live nearby, so they're on campus pretty late."

The College Prowler Take On...
Academics

A college cannot be considered one of the best in the world without attracting top-notch faculty. Most students are impressed with the collective knowledge and academic rigor of the professors. The major problems that Columbia students cite are the huge egos of the senior faculty and the lack of individual attention. If a student is sincere and persistent, however, it is possible to find stimulating mentors among the faculty. And do not disregard the old drunk—he may very well be the best professor you ever had. Columbia is the kind of place where you must find out who and what works for you.

Sometimes students have little choice in selecting a professor, especially if a course is offered only once a year. In those situations, you just have to bite the bullet. Students can ask around or use CULPA to learn about a specific professor. Many view the first week of school as a tasting menu. They go from course to course in order to find the professor who best fills their needs and sometimes they may even find an inspiring mentor in the process. Some students find their niche in their selected curriculum, while others are equally impressed by the diversity offered within the core requirements. One can find something of interest in a classroom at Columbia, but it takes more effort than just glancing through the course catalogue.

The College Prowler™ Grade on
Academics: A-

A high Academics grade generally indicates that professors are knowledgeable, accessible, and genuinely interested in their students' welfare. Other determining factors include class size, how well professors communicate, and whether or not classes are engaging.

Local Atmosphere

The Lowdown On...
Local Atmosphere

Region:
Northeast

City, State:
New York, New York

Setting:
Big City!

Distance from Philly:
2 hours

Distance from DC:
3.5 hours

Points of Interest:
Times Square
Broadway
SoHo
Harlem
Wall Street
The list goes on...

→

Closest Movie Theatres:

Loews Cineplex
Lincoln Square
1998 Broadway
(212) 50-LOEWS

Loews Cineplex Harlem USA
2309 Frederick Douglass Boulevard
(212) 665-6923

Clearview Metro Twin
2626 Broadway
212-505-3463.

Loews Cineplex 84th Street
2310 Broadway
(212) 50-LOEWS

Major Sports Teams:

Knicks (basketball)
Nets (basketball)
Rangers (hockey)
Islanders (hockey)
Mets (baseball)
Yankees (baseball)
Giants (football)
Jets (football)

Closest Shopping:

There's a K-Mart at 34th Street for general dormy stuff and a Macy's there as well, when you're ready to move on to furnishing your closet. There is every kind of store in Manhattan, but reliably a Gap on just about every other corner.

City Websites

http://www.newyork.citysearch.com.

Did You Know?

Five Fun Facts about New York:

1. Two of its many nicknames are The Big Apple and The City that Never Sleeps
2. It used to be called New Amsterdam
3. New York City has 722 miles of subway track
4. The New York Post was founded in 1803 by Alexander Hamilton and is the oldest newspaper in the United States
5. George Washington was sworn in to the presidency in New York City. Back then, it was the capital of the United States of America.

Local Slang:

The subway is referred to as New Yorkers by the train. That's all you need to know.

Famous People from New York City:

Kareem Abdul-Jabbar

Humphrey Bogart

Theodore Roosevelt

Barbra Streisand

Edith Wharton

Vince Lombardi

Students Speak Out On...
Local Atmosphere

"Manhattan itself is a vast playground with hip jazz clubs, trendy bars, low-key coffee shops, and charming restaurants featuring every imaginable type of cuisine. And then there is the typical New York touristy stuff like the museums, Times Square and Central Park."

Q "I do not like the atmosphere of Morningside Heights. It is **stuffy and overcrowded** with too many screaming children and stroller moms. Get out into the real New York away from the Upper West Side or Morningside Heights. Alphabet City, St. Mark's Place, the NYU area, Greenwich Village, TriBeCa, Soho, etc. all of it makes up a thriving, exciting, diverse atmosphere. You can see all of the movies, concerts, ballets, dance performances--anything you can imagine, it is is a wonderful city and there is nothing like New York."

Q "One of the hottest cities in the world. Stuff to stay away from? **Homeless people that don't perform on subway.** We are in a recession, after all. You should give your money to talented people."

Q "New York has got to be one of the **greatest cities on Earth.** There are several other universities in Manhattan and thousands of other young people also populate the surrounding areas. Columbia is located in an exciting city that has a lot to offer. Steer clear of the trends and try to visit the Met as often as possible."

Q "Dude, **it's New York**."

Q "Here's a valuable New York survival tip: if you ever see a crowd running away from something, **don't be an individual,** join the crowd and get out of the street and run away with them!"

Q "What? New York City? Figure it out for yourself, **it is what you make of it** and that takes effort but it's all worth it."

Q "Columbia is located in the relatively quiet Morningside Heights neighborhood of NYC. **It is a great place to sleep and study** before heading downtown on the weekend!"

Q "You really need to do research if you don't know what is available in New York City. **It is truly an amazing city!** There are Broadway shows, museums, great people, etc."

Q "**It's New York City. Isn't that enough said?** There's New York University downtown, and there are tons of things to do over there in the village such as museums and clubs. You name it; New York has it."

Q "The campus is beautiful, and you will have so much fun on and off campus. **You have the whole city to travel.**"

Q "I love living in New York because **you can taste and see all levels of status.** You can walk off of the campus after getting a bad grade on a test and see a man begging for food and remember how lucky you are; it just keeps things in perspective."

Q "There are tons of things to do in New York City, especially if you have the **willpower, money, or the right people** with you."

The College Prowler Take On...
Local Atmosphere

New York City has something for everyone and it does not take much for the staunchest suburbanite to find their niche somewhere in Manhattan. Some students rarely leave the Morningside Heights campus and consider it to be their home. The immediate area is full of restaurants, shops, bars and cafes so those who stay close to Columbia do have access to a slice of New York's offerings, though it's clear that the rest of the city offers many more diversions for the more adventurous souls.

The urban locale is part of the draw for many Columbia students, but those who prefer the quiet life can find comfort in some of the other geographic regions within the city. The trendy hipsters flock to Soho or Williamsburg in Brooklyn. Art lovers have the galleries in Chelsea and those wishing to catch the newest play have Broadway and off-Broadway and off-off Broadway at their disposal. There's always the Village, Central Park and midnight walks across the Brooklyn Bridge. After a little exploring, it is possible for anyone to find their happy place somewhere in New York. Sometimes students feel like the city is going to eat them alive, but after making some friends and getting to know the environment, New York City becomes more inviting and less scary for those unfamiliar with the uber-urban life.

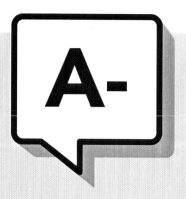

The College Prowler™ Grade on

Local Atmosphere: A-

A high Local Atmosphere grade indicates that the area surrounding campus is safe and scenic. Other factors include nearby attractions, proximity to other schools, and the town's attitude toward students

Safety & Security

The Lowdown On...
Safety & Security

Columbia Police:
(212) 854-7777

Safety Services:
Blue phones
Escort services

Health Services:
Basic medical services
Women's health office
Counseling and psychological services
Free HIV testing

Did You Know?

Columbia has a world-famous health web site called Go Ask Alice! (http://www.goaskalice.columbia.edu) where thousands of questions written by real people are answered by Columbia's health experts.

Health Center Office Hours:
- Monday-Thursday: 8 a.m.-6 p.m.
- Friday 8 a.m.-5 p.m.
- Closed on Sundays, but there is a physician on-call at all times.

Students Speak Out On...
Safety & Security

"The campus itself is like a citadel. There are only a few ways to enter the fortress-like facilities at Columbia University which makes it feel like its own little island village."

Q "Although the campus and the surrounding area are **very safe**, it is wise to be aware of your environment."

Q "It is very safe. On many early mornings I have wandered in a half-assed state around the campus at 4 a.m. and even been able to eat at Ollie's across the street and continue my life as it were daytime. The only thing is **avoid taking the subway between the hours of 2 and 7 a.m.** because frankly it is taking too much of a risk, but even that I have done."

Q "Columbia is the **safest place in New York City.**"

Q "**I have always felt safe** on campus despite being in NYC on September 11th."

Q "The campus feels pretty safe during the day, but **if you don't keep an eye on your stuff you will get robbed.** The nearby parks are not safe at night, and the usual threat of being female at college is there."

Q "Security and safety are **not issues at all.** I feel completely safe walking by myself in the wee hours of the morning around campus."

Q "It's very safe on campus, and **the NYPD takes great care of the rest of the city.**"

Q "Strangely enough, although Columbia is an open campus, I have always found it to be **extremely safe.** They close the main gates at 116th Street after a certain hour, and a security guard is posted 24/7. It's a pretty small campus, and while Morningside Heights was pretty sketchy 10 years ago, it's really cleaned up. I mean, I've definitely walked home at like four or five in the morning by myself ... no problem!"

Q "Security on campus is pretty tight. **They always have guards doing rounds**, and they always check up on visitors at the dorms."

Q "**I carry pepper spray everywhere** in New York City."

Q "Security seems to be good. **There are escorts that drive you home if you live off campus** and need to go home late. There are guards at the gates to enter the campus. Just so you know, Columbia borders Harlem, but it is really safe."

Q "Campus **safety is one of the best things about Columbia.** No matter where you are on campus, there are people and officers there. Also, there are security guards stationed in every building, and the campus is well-lighted."

Q "Well, New York is New York. I am not saying you are going to get mugged the minute you walk out of your dorm room, but **it is important to be wary of what is going on around you.** I believe Columbia has 24-hour security on campus and in the dorms; I feel very safe going there."

Q "Security is okay on campus, but pretty much **anyone can get inside if they know how.**"

Q "Safety is fine. **You just need to follow some really common sense rules,** and you will be fine. I really love the neighborhood. We have a campus, and the surrounding area is fairly residential."

Q "Campus **security and safety is great.** When you walk through the gates, you walk into a totally different world. I have never felt unsafe on or around campus. It is very busy in addition to being well-patrolled pretty much all the time."

Q "Security is fairly good. **I'm never really scared to walk around campus by myself at nighttime.** When I feel stressed and like I need some air, I always head out for a walk around campus, even if it's 2 a.m."

Q "There is a safe haven program where various shops and such around the area can call Columbia directly to get you an escort back to campus should you ever feel uneasy about heading back on your own. **You can call for an escort at any point if you don't feel it's safe** for you to return by yourself."

Q "The campus itself has **many precautions.** You have to use your Columbia ID to get into most places on campus, particularly the library, Lerner Hall (the student center), and any dormitory. Anyone who doesn't have an ID has to be signed in otherwise."

Q "Security is everywhere on campus. **You hear about more crimes from students than you do from neighborhood people,** but then again, if you're drunk and wandering around the sketchy streets at 3 a.m., you're just asking for trouble."

Q "Despite any fears your parents might have, **Columbia is extremely safe.** Yes, Harlem is next door, but there's nothing unsafe about it. Even former President Bill Clinton hangs out there—his office is in Harlem on 125th Street. Bars are open late, and dining establishments that cater to drunk students are open even later. On non-school nights, there are numerous students stumbling down Broadway drunk, and they would probably be really easy to jump or rob. Does it ever happen? Probably, but it has never happened to anyone I know."

Q "There are literally cop cars parked on every other block. Seriously. **There are NYPD squad cars with two policemen in them.** They aren't there to bust underage drinkers; they are there to make sure all the students, many of whom are sons and daughters of rich kids, stay safe. You don't have to worry about safety."

The College Prowler Take On...
Safety & Security

Most students feel safe at Columbia. It would be difficult not to, since Columbia security and the NYPD have such a high profile on campus. While it is possible for almost anyone to get on campus, access to certain buildings and all residence halls is restricted to those with a Columbia ID card. With escort services and emergency phones available, campus security excels at keeping students safe.

Simple common sense and street smarts are necessary to survive in any urban environment. Always be aware of your surroundings and avoid dodgy places at night, especially the local parks. Trusting your instincts will often protect you—if you feel unsafe, it's best to get out of the situation you're in. Fortunately, there are plenty of police and security guards around Columbia to provide assistance in such a predicament. Even though the area surrounding the school has been gentrified, there are still some sketchy areas that should be avoided at night. You don't want to make the mistake of getting on the wrong train and ending up in Harlem in the middle of the night. As safe as Columbia is, it is not a fortress void of any criminals. Keep your wits about you and keep your distance from the local panhandlers. Most are harmless, but you never know.

B

The College Prowler™ Grade on

Safety & Security: B

A high grade in Safety & Security means that students generally feel safe, campus police are visible, blue-light phones and escort services are readily available, and safety precautions are not overly necessary.

Computers

The Lowdown On...
Computers

High-Speed Network?
Yes

Wireless Network?
Yes

Number of Labs:
6

Numbers of Computers:
500

Operating Systems:
Mac
PC
Unix

→

24-Hour Labs:

Lerner Hall
Butler Library
Hartley
Carman
River
McBain
East Campus
Wien
Furnald
Broadway
Schapiro

Free Software:

Secure telnet and
file-transfer programs
EndNote
Symantec AntiVirus

Discounted Software:

MapInfo
MATLAB
Mathematica
SAS
SPSS
Stata

Charge to Print?

Undergraduates receive 100 free printed pages each week.

Did You Know?

At Columbia, students are given a University Network ID or UNI, which is usually their initials and some combination of numbers, and it is their email address and login to all computers. Students at Columbia, nerdy till the end, often jokingly refer to each other by their UNIs (hey, jfg32! Get over here!)

Students Speak Out On...
Computers

"Here, I would say that it depends on your major. The labs are big, and there is usually space, but if you are going to do English or poly sci or something where you will have to write a lot of papers, you should bring your own."

Q "Having not owned a computer for my first year at Columbia, I can say with some authority, **bring or buy a computer, even if it's a dinosaur.** The worst thing is having to run to campus at 4 a.m. to finish a paper in a packed room then realizing that others procrastinated as much as you."

Q "I think it is best to **bring a computer**, but computer labs in less populated dorms are well-kept secrets and virtually always available."

Q "The **computer labs are great**, though at times overcrowded. But most people respect the quiet rule (take all of your cell phone conversations outside) which they do not respect in the library. You definitely need your own computer in order to survive here."

Q "The network is an **embarrassment to higher education**."

Q "I'd bring my own computer because it makes life a lot easier. **Computer labs are really crowded during exams** and midterms, but there are also a bunch of computer labs that students don't generally go to. For example, Mudd is generally emptier than Butler Library."

Q "Computer labs are **crowded during the day,** but if you don't mind waiting, computer access is not a problem. The limited number of Macs on campus is not good, but the fact that they are not always operational can really be a problem. That written, there are plenty of working PCs. However, the same cannot be said about the campus printers. There are about two printers in each computer lab and it is rare for both (or even one) to be working properly. Expect long lines for printers."

Q "Finding space in a lab is usually easy, but bring your own computer. I **got by without my own printer but the network printing system isn't always that convenient.** The network is fast but bandwidth restrictions can mess you up for no reason (like if your roommate is on KaZaa all day, your account can suffer)."

Q "**Having your own computer is a must for convenience and academic sanity.** There are plenty of computers available on campus but the last thing you want to do is put all of your faith in being able to concentrate at the lab while pulling an all-nighter for a paper that's due the next morning."

Q "Yes, you definitely should bring your own computer and printer. It's just easier than always having to scout for an open terminal. There are various computer labs on campus, but **it's almost always a lot of stress** to locate one that's actually available."

Q "The computer labs are good and not always crowded because students bring their own computers. If you do bring your own computer, you have **access to the internet in your room.**"

Q "Most people have their own computers. **I'd suggest having one, but computer labs usually have room in them**, so it's really just a convenience thing."

Q "**Bring your own computer for sure**—you'll want it for AOL Instant Messenger."

Q "There are computer labs in every building, and **in some buildings, there are two or three labs**. Many of them stay open for 24 hours, but I prefer my own PC. It's better to have one in your room so that at any hour of the day you can do your work without walking to the lab."

Q "**The Ethernet connection in all the dorms is awesome.** It definitely beats my dial-up connection at home. There are plenty of labs around campus that you can access, but it's also pretty convenient to have your own computer."

Q "The computer network is great. **It's fast and convenient.** The labs are sometimes crowded. The printers are out of paper sometimes. You could get by without your own computer. People do that. But it's more convenient to have your own, especially during those last minutes before a paper is due when you just need to print something out and the printer in the lab is either crowded or broken or out of paper! Personally, I would rather have my own."

Q "**You definitely don't need your own computer,** but if you do decide to get one, get a laptop. I learned the hard way this year that laptops are so much better than desktops. You really don't need them because the school is well equipped with computer labs. However, if you don't have one, you'll miss out on the best part of college—AIM and downloading from Morpheus or KaZaa."

The College Prowler Take On...
Computers

While it is possible to survive at Columbia without a computer, it is not recommended. There are plenty of computer rooms around campus and also terminals for a quick look at your e-mail, but they are usually packed during the day and the waits are incredibly long at crunch times. The Barnard Library is one of the less populated options, and there are other rooms off the beaten path in the departments or other libraries that tend to be less crowded. The printers are not always reliable and it often becomes necessary to send a document to multiple locations, just hoping that one machine is working properly.

Procrastinators should definitely bring their own computer to school, even if it's just a dinosaur with a word processing unit. Many students wait until the last minute to finish (or start) a paper only to discover that this was not an original idea. Furthermore, as more professors learn how to incorporate the Internet into their courses, it's much more pleasant to read lectures notes or download the next problem set in your room while wearing pajamas than it is to scout around for an open computer and a functioning printer.

The College Prowler™ Grade on
Computers: B

A high grade in Computers designates that computer labs are available, the computer network is easily accessible, and the campus' computing technology is up-to-date.

Facilities

The Lowdown On...
Facilities

Student Center:
Lerner Hall

Athletic Center:
Marcellus Hartley Dodge
Fitness Center
Levien Gym
Uris Pool.

Libraries:
20

Popular Places to Chill:
Lerner Hall
The Hungarian Pastry Shop
Butler Library's undergraduate
reading rooms

What Is There to Do On Campus?

What isn't there to do? There's campus theater, frisbee golf, a cappella, and tons of places on and around campus to grab a bite to eat or something to drink.

Movie Theatre on Campus?

Yes. Roone Arledge Theater, Lerner Hall.

Bar on Campus?

No.

Coffeehouse on Campus?

No.

Bowling on Campus?

No.

Students Speak Out On...
Facilities

{ **"The facilities are beautiful. No other campus in NYC rivals it. And it is one of the only places in New York where grass is present. The gym is crowded but nice. Truly the best place on campus to spot hotties."**

Q "The libraries are staffed by people who actually know what they are doing and the stacks are well-maintained. **The media centers can be crowded**, especially in the course reserve section. If you have to watch a video for a class, watch it early because there are usually only one or two copies on reserve."

Q "An area that receives constant complaints at Butler Library (the main library on campus) is the digital editing equipment. There are only two stations for the entire undergraduate population and there is **a two-hour limit per session**. This makes it very difficult to finish film projects."

Q "Lerner Hall, the student center on campus, is the only building that does not look like it belongs here. In a community of brick and ivy stands this **awkward glass structure** that houses cafes, computer rooms, theaters and general meeting space. Once you get past the offbeat design of this place, you can enjoy the social atmosphere."

Q "The gym needs a little work but **it gets the job done.** Lerner isn't much of a student center, it's a ridiculous waste of space and really inaccessible and uncomfortable compared with other student unions I've visited."

Q "The facilities are a very nice and beautiful too. Everything is state of the art and **adorned in an amalgamation of Greco-Roman classicism**. Forget about the Gothic embellishments of Princeton and the University of Chicago, we've got Ancient Athens."

Q "The facilities are pretty good. The student center is new, but it's controversial as to whether it's good or not. I don't care for it all that much, but hey, that's just me."

Q "The athletic center is awesome, but, **it can be crowded during peak hours**. Lerner is pretty cool; it's the most interesting building you'll see on campus! You can study there, get some food, and meet up with people."

Q "On-campus facilities are pretty good. Computer labs are good. The fitness center is **awesome once you figure out how the heck to get around there**. The student center is a pain to get around, but everything is there."

Q "There's a new student center, but they're still learning how to use it and get good events in there. The gym is on campus and very active; depending on when you go, it can be very crowded or empty. **We could use some more facilities**, though. The computers are always kept up-to-date and are all over the place."

Q "The facilities are good, and they are making improvements constantly. The student center is brand new, the gym has extended hours and is expanding, and computers are everywhere. **Classrooms are well-equipped,** and libraries are nice spots to meet with teachers and classmates. The libraries are well-lit, comfortable, and plentiful!"

Q "The work-out room kind of sucks; I highly advise you to **get a membership at Wellbridge Fitness Club instead**, if you have the money. They have a hot tub and a pool."

Q "The athletic center boasts **an impressive layout** and everything else is satisfactory."

Q "There's a pretty good-sized gym with lots of weights, cardio machines, basketball courts, and pretty much everything else you can think of. The gym can be kind of crowded, though, and you usually have to sign up in advance for a cardio machine. At peak times, the weight room can be quite crowded, too. There's **a new student center** that was built about three years ago that has lots of stuff in it like student mail services, restaurants, computer labs, auditoriums, and a movie theater. Overall, I'd say the facilities on campus are pretty decent, although some of the classrooms are still kind of old."

The College Prowler Take On...
Facilities

The city provides plenty of alternatives for those who wish to study or socialize off campus (with the Hungarian Pastry Shop being a favorite). That said, sooner or later you will need to visit one or more of the campus libraries. The 20 or so libraries are usually full, especially Butler, but even during finals, it is possible to find a quiet corner to do some studying and the staff is generally knowledgeable and helpful. Students have been critical of the media centers located within the libraries, but with a little planning, you can get what you need from these facilities. Many course books are held on reserve at the library, but they are not allowed to leave the building for more than a few hours so good planning is essential to getting your hands on the materials you require.

Lerner Hall has cafes, computer labs, a bank, a copy center, mailboxes, club meeting spaces, music rooms and theaters to serve the student populace. Although the modern architecture does not match the rest of the campus, the building itself is useful and the people are accommodating. Many students consider the gym as one of the best things about the campus. Even though it is often crowded, it is well-maintained and also serves as a good place to people watch. It even boasts an indoor pool and track. Lockers are rented on a first-come, first-serve basis and the demand always exceeds the supply.

B-

The College Prowler™ Grade on
Facilities: B-

A high Facilities grade indicates that the campus is aesthetically pleasing and well-maintained; facilities are state-of-the-art, and libraries are exceptional. Other determining factors include the quality of both athletic and student centers and an abundance of things to do on campus.

Campus Dining

The Lowdown On...
Campus Dining

Freshman Meal Plan Requirement?

Yes

Meal Plan Average Cost:

$3,456 per year

Places to Grab a Bite with Your Meal Plan:

Blue Java Coffee Bar, Butler Library

Sunday, 12 p.m.-11 p.m.
Monday – Thursday, 8 a.m.-11 p.m. Friday, 8 a.m.-9 p.m.
Saturday, 12 p.m.-6 p.m.

A life-saving coffee corner when it's getting late and you know you'll need a boost to study for a few more hours. They also have little munchies if you missed out on a meal because you were mired in mathematics

Café (212),
Lerner Hall

Monday-Thursday, 8 a.m.-2 a.m. Friday, 8 a.m.-9 p.m. Saturday, 9 a.m.-9 p.m. Sunday, 9 a.m.-2 a.m.

Salads and sandwiches, a chaotic place to get food as it's in the entrance to Lerner, next ot the ATMs, and always full. But they often have good soup in the winter, so it's worth looking into.

Carleton Lounge,
Mudd Hall

Monday – Friday, 10 a.m.-4 p.m.

A little stop off for chips or coffee before hitting the lab.

Ferris Booth Commons,
Lerner Hall

Monday-Thursday, 7:30 a.m. - 9:00 p.m. Friday: 7:30 a.m. - 6:00 p.m.

Stirfry, wraps, sushi, a little more upscale and a nice place to sit with friends or study.

Food Court,
Wien Hall

Monday-Friday, 11 a.m.-6:30 p.m.

Taco Bell, Pizza Hut, and the like make this a good choice when you need grease, really fast.

Hartley Kosher Deli,
Hartley Hall

Monday – Thursday, 11 a.m.-2 p.m.

Good food that's also kosher.

JJ's Place,
John Jay Hall

Monday – Thursday, 8 pm-2 a.m. Saturday, 1 p.m.-8 p.m. Sunday, 1 p.m.-2 a.m.

Greasy chicken fingers and other freshman fifteen delicacies. Bonus: it has a sort of supermarket style part, if you want to pick up something that's more foodlike.

John Jay Dining Hall

Monday-Sunday, 10:30 a.m. - 1:30 p.m, 5 p.m.-8 p.m.

Everything you could think of to serve for dinner, and a lot of things that never crossed your mind. As a freshman, this will be dinner, so be thankful that you can choose between Lucky Charms and Corn Pops every night.

Lenfest Café,
Jerome Greene Hall

Monday – Friday, 8:30 a.m.-4 p.m.

Salads and sandwiches.

Uris Deli, Uris Hall

Monday-Wednesday, 7:30 a.m.-7 p.m. Thursday-Friday, 7:30 a.m.-5 p.m.

Great sandwiches and a nice coffee bar too.

Off-Campus Places to Use Your Meal Plan:

None

24-Hour On-Campus Eating?

None

Student Favorites:

Uris Hall

Ferris Booth Commons

Other Options:

All the restaurants, from Mexican to Japanese to Indian, deliver to your door.

Did You Know?

Furnald Hall used to have a pub in it (called Furnald Pub), but the first floor is now a beautiful lounge with hardwood floors and couches where a cappella groups often perform and residents study.

Students Speak Out On...
Campus Dining

{ **"Unfortunately, the near impossibility of decent off-campus housing combined with the disappointing kitchens located in the dorms make it difficult to cook for yourself in the dorms. Bring a lot of money to eat out."**

Q "Lerner Hall has the best soup to warm you up on a cold winters' day. **The lines suck and sandwiches and sushi are seriously overpriced**, but they are tasty. The dining halls have good salad bars, but the hot food is not always appetizing."

Q "The food is very good. **There is nothing to complain about in the slightest.** However, the dining plans are outrageously expensive. For the price that you pay there you could eat at a pretty nice restaurant every day. Eat out, it is more convenient and also faster. Plus, there are so many places to choose from. The sandwich place in cafe 212 is really good, and their lunch specials are also good."

Q "During your first year at Columbia, they make you enroll in a meal plan that includes cafeteria food at John Jay. All I can say is that **you should pick the meal plan with the least amount of meals but more points.** The food is not that bad though, I actually had no problems with the food, and if you don't want to eat at the cafeteria in John Jay, we have about five other cafeterias that have better food."

Q "Food on campus is fine. **Best food can be found in Uris Hall** (the Business School). Not very junk food heavy, so it's unlikely that you'll gain the 'Freshman 15.'"

Q "**Save your money to eat downtown on the weekends.** Manhattan is rich with culinary delights for the Epicurean in all of us."

Q "Dining hall food is the same as anywhere. **212 is a great place for sandwiches** and Ferris Booth features healthier dining options like fresh fish with vegetable side dishes."

Q "The dining hall is bad, I admit. **The places where you can swipe your Columbia Card to use dining points are great.** There's stir-fry, sushi, sandwiches, and Pizza Hut. You can get pretty much anything you want."

Q "The first-year meal plans at Columbia are terrible. **They are way overpriced for what you get.** Get the meal plan with the fewest meals and the most points, trust me. However, after the first year, most students opt out of the plans and just put dining dollars on their student cards."

Q "No complaints. John Jay is the dining hall. **212 is a good campus cafe.** There are some other spots on campus to grab some food, too—Hewitt, Mac, and Java City."

Q "On campus, **food is okay**, and there is a new place to eat in the new student center called Ferris Booth Commons, which is nice. Also, the grad schools have good places to get food, like Uris at the business school—I always eat there."

Q "You really shouldn't have any high expectations where that is concerned. Granted, **the food isn't the worst in the world, but it's far from high-quality.** John Jay dining hall is definitely not my favorite place to eat, but it's convenient. There are other delis and cafeterias on campus that are actually pretty decent if you want a sandwich or a quick bite to eat."

The College Prowler Take On...
Campus Dining

Freshmen are required to have dining plans during their first year at Columbia and there is only one dining hall on campus where they can eat breakfast and dinner (lunch is purchased with points at eateries mentioned above). Conventional wisdom suggests that students should invest in the meal package with the fewest meals and the most points. While few sing the praises of cafeteria food, it is even rarer for students to totally disparage the grub at Columbia either. The dining hall food is OK and the on-campus cafes have a little something for everyone.

Sophomores and upperclassmen who go off meal plans often voice regrets about not being able to have food at their fingertips, but many rectify this problem by getting a Flex Account. This allows students to use their Columbia ID to buy food without having to worry about having cash on them. One benefit of eating meals on campus with a card is that it is tax-free, so one saves a lot of money by using points to pick up a snack on campus; the cafes in Lerner Hall and Uris are among the student favorites for sandwiches, soups or coffee breaks.

The College Prowler™ Grade on
Campus Dining:
D+

Our grade on Campus Dining addresses the quality of both school-owned dining halls and independent on-campus restaurants as well as the price, availability, and variety of food.

Off-Campus Dining

The Lowdown On...
Off-Campus Dining

Restaurant Prowler:
Popular Places to Eat!

Caffé Taci
Food: Italian

Address: 2841 Broadway

Phone: (212) 678-5345

Cool Features: Live opera every Wednesday and Saturday night

Hours: Sunday-Thursday 10 a.m.-12:30 p.m. Friday-Sat 10 a.m.-1 a.m.

Price: $20 and under per person

Deluxe
Food: American

Address: 2896 Broadway

Phone: (212) 662-7900

Cool Features: Great weekend brunch, for when the dining hall is not enough.

Price: $20 and under per person

Hours: Monday-Thursday 7 a.m.-12 a.m., Friday 7 a.m.-1 a.m., Saturday 8 a.m.-1 a.m., Sunday: 8 a.m.-midnight

➜

Dynasty

Food: Chinese

Address: 2836 Broadway

Phone (212) 665-6455

Cool Features: Chinese food!

Price $20 and under per person

Hours: Monday-Friday 11:30am to 11:30pm, Saturday-Sunday 11:30 a.m.-midnight

The Heights

Food: American

Address: 2867 Broadway

Phone: (212) 866-7035

Cool Features: margaritas

Price: $10 and under per person

Hours: Monday-Thursday 11:30 a.m.-12 a.m., Friday 11:30 a.m.-1 a.m., Saturday 11 a.m.-1 a.m., Sunday 11 a.m.-12 a.m.

Koronet Pizzeria

Food: Italian

Address: 2848 Broadway

Phone: (212) 222-1566

Cool Features: The absolute biggest slice of pizza you've ever seen (or attempted to eat)

Price: $10 and under per person

Hours: Monday-Sunday, 9 a.m.-2 a.m.

Max SoHa

Food: Italian

Address: 1274 Amsterdam Avenue

Phone: (212) 531-2221

Cool Features: Good Italian food slightly off the beaten Columbia track

Price: $30 and under per person

Hours: Seven days a week 11:30 a.m.-11:30 p.m.

Le Monde

Food: French

Address: 2885 Broadway

Phone: (212) 531-3939

Cool Features: great French décor!

Price: $30 and under per person

Hours: Monday–Thursday 11:30 am-12:30 am, Friday 11:30 am-1:30 am, Saturday 10:30 am-1:30 am, Sunday 10:30 am-12:30 am

Symposium

Food: Greek

Address: 544 West 113th Street

Phone: (212) 865-1011

Cool Features: the sweet staff and sweet, sweet sangria

Price: $20 and under per person

Hours: Monday-Sunday 12pm-11pm.

Tomo

Food: Japanese

Address: 2850 Broadway

Phone: (212) 665-2916

Cool Features: great lunch specials on sushi

Price: $15 and under per person

Hours: Seven days a week, noon-11.30 p.m.

Tom's Restaurant

Food: American

Address: 2880 Broadway

Phone: (212) 864-6137

Hours: Sunday-Wednesday 6 a.m.-1:30 a.m. Thursdasy-Saturday 24 hours.

Cool Features: before you go inside, you can look at the sign and pretend you're on Seinfeld. Then you can stop acting like a dork and eat lunch.

Price: $10 and under per person

The West End

Food: Burgers and Fries

Address: 2911 Broadway

Phone: (212) 662-8830

Cool Features: Happy hour 4-7

Price: $10 and under per person

Hours: Mon-Sun 11am-3am.

The Wrapp Factory

Food: Wraps, American

Address 2857 Broadway

Phone: (212) 665-5870

Cool Features: Tons of wraps to choose from and great smoothies as an added bonus.

Price: $10 and under per person

Hours: Monday-Sunday, 12 p.m.-10 p.m.

Best Pizza:

Koronet's

Best Chinese:

Dynasty

Best Breakfast:

Tom's Restaurant

Best Wings:

The West End

Best Healthy:

The Wrapp Factory

Best Place to Take Your Parents:

Le Monde

Closest Grocery Store

University Food Market

2943 Broadway

Phone: (212) 666-4190

Did You Know?

Late-Night, Half-Price Food Specials
None (they're not big on cheap things in New York).

24-Hour Eating
On the weekend, Tom's Restaurant.

Fun Facts

The exterior of Tom's appears in Seinfeld, so watch out for tourists taking photos in front of it, but don't expect the inside to look the same as on TV—they use a different location for the interior.

Koronet's serves pizza slices as big as your head (no, actually bigger), till four a.m. A great place to stop on your way home. From the library, I mean.

Student Favorites

- The West End
- The Heights
- Caffé Taci
- Symposium
- Le Monde
- Tom's Restaurant
- Tomo

Students Speak Out On...
Off-Campus Dining

> "Remember that Columbia is in New York City, where you can get virtually any type of food you want at any time of the day."

Q "There are some **great little places around the area** that have good stuff. Koronet's serves huge slices of pizza for cheap ($2-3), there's an Ollie's across Broadway for Chinese-American, Tomo for Japanese down the road, Pinnacle has pizza and sandwiches, and there's the Milano Market, the Korean Mill, P&W and the Hungarian Pastry Shop on Amsterdam. There is a bunch more, and they're all in walking distance. Of course, if you're feeling adventurous enough you can always hop on the subway and try out other restaurants around the city."

Q "There are about **20 restaurants within a few blocks of campus.** Lunch specials abound with Caffe Swish being among the best with its tasty Asian fusion cuisine and lousy service. There are sandwich shops, pizza parlors and diners available for quick bites. The West End is probably the most popular place to eat. It's only a block or two away from school and it offers a little bit of everything from bar food to Mexican eats, as well as French and Italian dishes."

Q "The food in New York City is great! **You can find anything you want.** I love Go Sushi! If you want names, just go to a nightlife website."

Q "The area around Columbia is adorable, and there is everything you can imagine **from Ethiopian to French.** There's Thai, Chinese, falafel, bagels, and coffee shops. It's really a great area."

Q "Anyplace in New York City has to be good or else it won't survive. **There are so many great places within a few blocks or a short subway ride away.** Presto's is a great Italian place. Sophia's is another Italian place that is cheaper and has great Monday night specials. Mama Mexico's is awesome; it's down a bit farther but worth the walk. Koronet's has great cheap and huge pizza—I mean it's huge … something that you have to see for yourself! There is also Indian Cafe, a wrap place, and tons of Asian spots for take out or eat in. My favorite for take out Chinese is Empire Corner because it's yummy, quick, and pretty inexpensive!"

Q "New York City has some of the **best restaurants in the world.** Grab yourself a Zagat's guide and venture! Don't have much money? Head down to Gray's Papaya. Best hot dogs on the planet. Want to stay close to campus? Check out the new restaurant row on Amsterdam and 123rd (Max, Kitchenette, etc.)."

Q "The immediate neighborhood is **full of restaurants several of which are really lackluster**. For a good deal on a sushi lunch go to Tomo. For Southeast Asian fare Caffe Swish can't be beat. For an enormous slice of pizza, you've got Koronets. And for a little bit of relaxingly aloof service, there's Toast which serves an array of sturdy Americana dishes."

Q "They're really good places around Columbia, in my opinion. **There are some nice sit-down places, which I go to infrequently.** There are also lots of good pizza places and delis. Some good names include Koronet's, Famiglia's, The Wrapp Factory, Ollie's, and a lot more."

Q "Oh gosh! **There are so many!** And all are a lot of fun to go to. There's Le Monde, Deluxe, Tom's, Nacho Mama's, Nussbaum, Columbia Cottage, Cafe Pertutti, two supermarkets, two Starbucks, and who can forget AmCaf and West End—the Real World New York went there one episode."

Q "All the restaurants around the campus are excellent. **The diversity of the restaurants is awesome.**"

Q "Although the food in this part of town is good, **it's worthwhile to hop on the train and check out Negril on 23rd and 9th.** This is the best place to eat in New York. It is a Jamaican restaurant with spicy meals that hit the spot after a rough week of classes."

Q "There are lots of good restaurants in the area. **I am keen for salads, so I like the quick places like Strokos and Hamilton's.** Both have salads made to order and sandwiches. There are also good sit-down restaurants everywhere on Broadway, including Tom's Restaurant, which is the restaurant they always show on Seinfeld. My favorites are a French place called Le Monde, an Italian place called V&Ts, and a noodle shop called Ollie's."

Q "New York City is **filled with fabulous restaurants.** I can't even begin to explain all the wonderful cuisine in the entire city. You can find food from all over the world."

Q "Off campus, **there are a ton of places.** There's good Italian (Max's on 123rd and Amsterdam, or Taci, Pertutti), pretty good Chinese, and good Indian. Plus, of course there's Tom's Diner of Seinfeld fame."

Q "Tom's Restaurant (the one from the song by Susanne Vega and pictured in Seinfeld all the time) is one block from campus. **The Heights has really good food, and Le Monde has an amazing Belgian beer selection.** Things are pretty expensive at most of the places in the City, so I'm really not sure how the average Joe eats; we only get chicken and rice and beans."

The College Prowler Take On...
Off-Campus Dining

There are only a few places in the world that have such a wonderful variety of food as New York. Within just a few blocks of campus there are pizza places, sushi bars, Italian restaurants, diners, cafes and just about everything you can imagine. And that's just what's in the local neighborhood. Then there's the rest of the city.

Everyone has their own favorite local haunt, but the West End and Caffe Taci are two of the best. One special thing about New York is that almost every restaurant delivers until at least midnight, so you don't even have to leave your room to have some great food brought to your doorstep. For students on the go, there's always a local place to get a sandwich, wrap or a salad. Brunch is really big in New York, and although many hot spots are crowded, they are often worth the wait. Don't be afraid to experiment with ethnic cuisines. In this city, you can get what you want whenever you want it. As far as food goes, it does not get any better than New York City.

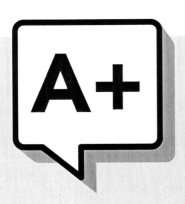

The College Prowler™ Grade on
Off-Campus
Dining: A+

A high off-campus dining grade implies that off-campus restaurants are affordable, accessible, and worth visiting. Other factors include the variety of cuisine and the availability of alternative options (vegetarian, vegan, Kosher, etc.).

Campus Housing

The Lowdown On...
Campus Housing

Best Dorms:
East Campus
Hogan
Ruggles

Worst Dorms:
Wien

Room Types:
Standard & suite-style

Number of Dormitories:
16

Undergrads on Campus:
98%

Students in:
Singles: 60%
Doubles: 34%
Apartments: 6%

Dormitory Residences:

Broadway

Floors: 10

Total Occupancy: 371

Bathrooms: four single-sex per floor

Co-Ed: Yes

Percentage of Men/Women: 50/50

Percentage of First-Year Students: 0%

Room Types: singles, doubles

Special Features: This brand-new building has three speedy elevators and two rooftop lounges for studying or holding meetings. Floor lounges have TVs, and each communal kitchen is equipped with a dishwasher. Added bonus: the building is within spitting distance of Lerner Hall, Butler Library, many academic buildings, and the restaurants and shops that line Broadway.

Carman

Floors: 13

Total Occupancy: 572

Bathrooms: One for every four people.

Co-Ed: Yes

Percentage of Men/Women: 50/50

Percentage of First-Year Students: 100%

Room Types: doubles

Carman (Continued)

Special Features: This freshman dorm bustles with activity all the time, as every first-year lives in a "suite"—two doubles next door that share a bathroom.

East Campus

Floors: 20

Total Occupancy: 742

Bathrooms: One for every two, five or six people, depending on what type of suite you live in.

Co-Ed: Yes

Percentage of Men/Women: 50/50

Percentage of First-Year Students: 10%

Room Types: Duplex suites with three singles and one double; flats with two singles; townhouses with five or six singles.

Special Features: East Campus is a popular dorm because of its diverse population—almost everyone at Columbia wants to live in these dishwasher-equipped suites that often have awesome high-rise views of the city (the roof is not to be believed. It's the best view of New York City in all of Manhattan). This year, freshman will also be living here, adding even more types of people to this populous residence hall.

Furnald

Floors: 10

Total Occupancy: 234

Bathrooms: One set of bathrooms on each floor

Co-Ed: Yes

Percentage of Men/Women: 50/50

Percentage of First-Year Students: 20%

Room Types: Singles and doubles.

Special Features: Formerly a senior dorm, Residential Life has now opened it up to underclassmen, so a few lucky freshman and sophomores get to enjoy living in the middle of all the action in probably the most beautiful residence hall on campus.

Hartley

Floors: 10

Total Occupancy: 231

Bathrooms: One in each suite.

Co-Ed: Yes

Percentage of Men/Women: 50/50

Percentage of First-Year Students: 60%

Room Types: Singles and doubles.

Special Features: With Wallach, Hartley forms the Learning and Living Center, known as the LLC. With regular events, this dorm offers more of a community-oriented experience for all its residents (who range from freshman to senior). Because of this, you must apply to live in the LLC.

Hogan

Floors: 7

Total Occupancy: 114

Bathrooms: One in each suite.

Co-Ed: Yes

Percentage of Men/Women: 50/50

Percentage of First-Year Students: 0%

Room Types: Singles

Special Features: If you ruled the world, you'd be a senior, living in this dorm, with your three best friends. With beautiful kitchens, huge singles, and a nice common room, Hogan is the top of the Columbia housing heap.

John Jay

Floors: 15

Total Occupancy: 459

Bathrooms: One set per floor.

Co-Ed: Yes

Percentage of Men/Women: 50/50

Percentage of First-Year Students: 100%

Room Types: Singles

Special Features: This freshman dorm is in the same building as the dining hall (ensuring all weekend trips to brunch are conducted in pajamas) and its residents enjoy the privacy of their singles, while still being able to socialize with their freshman floormates.

McBain

Floors: 8

Total Occupancy: 338

Bathrooms: One set per floor.

Co-Ed: Yes

Percentage of Men/Women: 50/50

Percentage of First-Year Students: 0%

Room Types: Mostly doubles, a few singles, some of which are huge.

Special Features: Sometimes referred to as Carman II, McBain is a sophomore dorm that often houses freshmen who lived in Carman during their first year, and has the same friendly feel.

River

Floors: 6

Total Occupancy: 127

Bathrooms: One in each suite, for five or six people.

Co-Ed: Yes

Percentage of Men/Women: 50/50

Percentage of First-Year Students: 0%

Room Types: singles.

Special Features: The seniors who didn't make it into Hogan often find residential happiness in this suite-style dorm that offers more apartment style living than underclassmen hall arrangements. Added bonus: it was recently renovated, with new bathrooms and kitchens, which include a half-dishwasher.

Ruggles

Floors: 8

Total Occupancy: 192

Bathrooms: One in each four-person suite, one and one half in the seven-person suites.

Co-Ed: Yes

Percentage of Men/Women: 50/50

Percentage of First-Year Students: 0%

Room Types: singles and doubles.

Special Features: Another favorite among upperclassmen for more suite-style living, Ruggles boasts free "John-Jay TV"—lucky residents can see directly across 114th Street into the freshman dorm, John Jay, for some entertainment on slow study nights.

Schapiro

Floors: 16

Total Occupancy: 417

Bathrooms: On lower more populous floors, two sets of single-sex bathrooms. On higher floors, only one set.

Co-Ed: Yes

Percentage of Men/Women: 50/50

Percentage of First-Year Students: 0%

Room Types: singles and doubles.

Schapiro (Continued)

Special Features: Schapiro is a no-nonsense place to get a single on a hall, with floor bathrooms and kitchens. Added bonus: a south facing room on floors 12-16 will give you a great view of Manhattan.

Wallach

Floors: 10

Total Occupancy: 237

Bathrooms: One in each suite.

Co-Ed: Yes

Percentage of Men/Women: 50/50

Percentage of First-Year Students: 60%

Room Types: singles and doubles.

Special Features: With Hartley, Wallach forms the Learning and Living Center, known as the LLC. With regular events, this dorm offers more of a community-oriented experience for all its residents (who range from freshman to senior). Because of this, you must apply to live in the LLC.

Watt

Floors: 6

Total Occupancy: 143

Bathrooms: One in each apartment.

Co-Ed: Yes

Percentage of Men/Women: 50/50

Percentage of First-Year Students: 0%

Room Types: studio, one bedroom and two bedroom apartments..

Special Features: This is the closest any Columbia student living on campus will get to real New York apartment life (without the cost!). Seniors who have the luckiest day of their life when lottery numbers are assigned can get a studio apartment—meaning their own kitchen and bathroom. Juniors and sophomores often sacrifice privacy for standard of living and share a one bedroom.

Bed Type
Twin extra long, some lofts and bunk beds.

Available for Rent
Refrigerators.

Cleaning Service?
In hall-style dorms, floor bathrooms are cleaned once a day. In suite-style dorms, bathrooms are cleaned once a week.

What You Get
A bed, a dresser, a chair, desk, a chest of drawers, ethernet access, a campus phone, and trash can. Cable service and upgraded phones are available at additional cost.

Also Available
Single sex floors are available in hall-style dorms, smoking is by floor (except first-year dormitories, which are all smoke-free), and special interest housing can be obtained through an application process.

Did You Know?

Columbia dorms are riddled with serious elevator etiquette. Because most buildings are tall, old, and have slow elevators, it is customary to walk one or two flights of stairs in lieu of taking the elevator. The same goes for walking one flight to the basement for laundry (though exceptions are made for coming up with a big bag of clothes and detergent). Those disobeying these unwritten laws of CU res life will be subjected to snide comments from fellow elevator riders accompanied by frequent button pushing to speed up the ride.

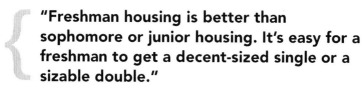

Students Speak Out On...
Campus Housing

"Freshman housing is better than sophomore or junior housing. It's easy for a freshman to get a decent-sized single or a sizable double."

Q "Living in the dorms is just fine. **Almost like living at home**, but smaller."

Q "I lived in John Jay my freshman year. **I highly recommend a single** if you can get it. There's just so much to be said for privacy. I had a huge single and loved every minute of it. Don't listen to those who tell you John Jay is antisocial. I've made some of my closest friends on my hall there."

Q "The dorms are **convenient and pleasant.** Which are "nice" is contingent on one's living style (single, suite, etc.)."

Q "As freshmen, we don't get much choice. I mean, I am not saying these dorms are shacks, but I am also not saying they are the Four Seasons Hotel. **I think they are just fine** from what I saw."

Q "The dorms are **hit and miss.** The apartment housing however is really much more hospitable and homey. If you're lucky you'll be placed in an apartment which doesn't look like much from the outside but that on the inside is beautifully well kept and refurbished."

Q "Furnald is the best freshmen dorm! It's so nice! **John Jay is tiny and lame**, and Carman's not that bad."

Q "Dorms are **kind of crappy.** The first-year and senior-year dorms are decent, though."

Q "Dorms are nice. **Columbia gives you singles if you want them.** I have actually lived in both of the freshmen dorms. Carman is known to be more social; I liked it a lot. But having a single is really sweet, so I'd honestly go for John Jay if I had to do it over."

Q "Depends what you want. But **chances are you won't get it.** Housing is getting worse, I hated my roommate and I hate the roommate I am about to have. John Jay is a prison for reclusive asocial freaks. Furnald has dorms that are way too nice for first years and even sophomores."

Q "Dorms are, **overall, pretty good.** I lived in John Jay my freshman year and loved it. I would have stayed in my little single forever. That tiny room becomes a palace; it's the best. Most of my floormates and friends in the building felt the same way; it's a great place to live, very social, and convenient to the dining hall, health services, the library, and Hamilton. You also have total privacy if you want to sleep, do work, or just chill out."

Q "Carman is a freshman favorite. If you want the roommate experience or have a tough time meeting people, then it is totally the dorm for you because you are guaranteed to know three people—your suitemates. Whatever you do, **don't go for a John Jay double**; you could get a walkthrough and those are nice, but you could get an L shape and those are not so nice, so don't risk it. For a double, pick Carman. Furnald is also a really nice dorm, though it's less social than the others because it is half sophomores."

Q "**Try for Furnald**, but for backup, go for Carman then John Jay. Unless you want to do the LLC (Hartley-Wallach), which is what I did—they are co-ed suites and I think they're the best."

Q "I say John Jay is the way to go, but that's only because I lived there. Wherever you live, you will hopefully think it is the better, cooler, nicer dorm. **People from Jay love Jay;** people from Carman love Carman; people from Furnald think that both of those suck and say that Furnald's the way to go. Good luck."

Q "The dorms really **vary in quality.** Housing is chosen based on seniority; however there are lots of restrictions and certain dorms are reserved for freshmen, etc. Except for sophomore year, most students are generally able to get singles for the rest of the other three years."

The College Prowler Take On...
Campus Housing

Columbia housing is not created equally. All Columbia College and SEAS freshmen are required to live on campus and the university saves decent living space for them. Once you have to undergo the housing lottery, you'd best hope that the housing gods are with you. Some suites are spacious with great views. Some singles are closets. There are as many sob stories as there are success ones. General Studies students are often housed in apartments together, though a housing shortage currently plagues all the undergraduate schools.

For Columbia College students living on campus, the dorms are small, but pretty good. Most students choose to stay on campus because there is no better deal in New York. Living with friends can sometimes improve a less than ideal situation, but others say that a small room is a small room. To get satisfactory housing, a sacrifice must be made. Generally, if you get space you have no privacy and if you have privacy, there's no space, but there are exceptions to this rule. For General Studies students, submitting your housing information on time is key to finding a suitable place to live and study while at Columbia. For undergraduates who are subjected to the lottery, often it's the luck of the draw (though during housing season, there are many, many Web sites with mathematical breakdowns of your chances of nailing a certain room based on the number you've drawn). Most Columbia students view the on-campus living situation as a character-building experience—you learn your limits of socialization and how to live with someone whose feng-shui differs ever so slightly from yours. Also, when all else fails, room transfers and off-campus housing are possible.

The College Prowler™ Grade on
Campus Housing:
C+

A high Campus Housing grade indicates that dorms are clean, well-maintained, and spacious. Other determining factors include variety of dorms, proximity to classes, and social atmosphere.

Off-Campus Housing

The Lowdown On...
Off-Campus Housing

Undergrads in Off-Campus Housing:
2%

Average Rent for a Studio:
$900/month

Average Rent for a One-Bedroom:
$1300/month

Average Rent for a Two-Bedroom:
$2200/month

Popular Areas:
Harlem
Washington Heights

Best Time to Look for a Place:
Right after you hit the lottery.

Students Speak Out On...
Off-Campus Housing

"Living in Manhattan is expensive! I would recommend living on campus or getting an apartment in another borough, like Brooklyn or Queens. But, if you aren't familiar with the city, live on campus."

Q "Not only is it very expensive to live in Manhattan but in order to find affordable housing off campus **you're going to have to resign yourself to some distant corner of the city**. Off-campus housing is rarely worth it because a long commute in the city everyday on your way to class will kill you."

Q "I live in Manhattan—20 blocks away from campus—and I still chose to live on campus. **Rent in New York City is super-expensive**, so if you're hoping to move off campus in an affordable place, it's going to be way uptown."

Q "You can definitely sublet an apartment off campus. However, **mostly everyone lives on campus**, as you're guaranteed housing for four years. A couple of my friends are renting apartments over the summer at decent prices."

Q "Expect to pay at least $1000 per month for a tiny studio apartment. **Sometimes you can luck out,** but it usually takes a few months to find a suitable space. Rental brokers are very expensive (10-20 percent of the first year's rent must be paid to these people who help you find an apartment) and it is difficult to find an apartment without one. Some students choose to live in cheaper areas of Manhattan or Brooklyn, but the commute makes this situation less than ideal for the busy student."

Q "I really don't know. **I dream of off campus housing.**"

Q "With the exception of Greek housing, **off-campus housing not convenient at all.**"

Q "**You're really not going to want to live off campus**, I don't think. But, there are dorms that are actually not in the main campus area. There's something for everyone."

Q "There is an office that helps you find an apartment off campus. **Columbia owns a lot of apartment buildings and the commute in New York is not bad**; you can also find a bus or train to get you back and forth."

Q "Off-campus housing is **tough to find**; I got lucky. It's expensive to live off campus."

Q "I'm sure that housing off campus is **pretty expensive.** I only know one person who lives off-campus, and his apartment costs him plenty more than my family can afford."

Q "**Live on campus.** Most housing is pretty good, except for sophomores with bad lottery numbers. I lived in a frat house sophomore and junior years. A new dorm was built two years ago called Broadway, and it is pretty nice and has air conditioning, so the housing situation is even better now."

Q "I don't know many people that live off campus. First of all, living in New York City is **very expensive**, and the dorms are actually pretty reasonably-priced. Most undergrads that live off campus probably either got kicked out of housing or were transfers."

The College Prowler Take On...
Off-Campus Housing

There are two words that strike fear into the hearts of those seeking an apartment to rent in New York, "broker's fee." A broker's fee is 10 to 20 percent of the first year's rent that gets paid to someone who has spent all of 15 minutes helping you find an apartment. It is difficult to find an apartment without a broker, but it is not impossible. Affordable off-campus housing is usually quite a commute from campus, but some find the extra privacy to be a benefit and use the commutes to study, but the majority end up wishing for a place nearer to campus. Most who live off-campus, but do not have a lengthy commute, seem happy with their decision to be apart from Columbia, but they often complain about the exorbitant rent and utility bills, not to mention the cost of furniture. Even Ikea can burn a hole in your wallet, but New Yorkers throw away some perfectly good items, so you can always furnish your place with egg crates and cinder blocks until you find some wooden shelves on the sidewalk.

Most leases are for a year, but some find subletting a useful alternative. Roommate wanted signs are posted all over the city and this can be a bit dangerous. At least with Columbia housing there is always someone to complain to. When you live with strangers off-campus you are on your own. Finding off-campus housing without a broker's fee requires money, patience and a little bit of luck. On-campus housing is easily the best rental deal in New York City, but you have to give up some autonomy.

The College Prowler™ Grade on

Off-Campus
Housing: F

A high grade in Off-Campus Housing indicates that apartments are of high quality, close to campus, affordable, and easy to secure.

Diversity

The Lowdown On...
Diversity

American Indian:
0%

Asian or Pacific Islander:
13%

African American:
9%

Hispanic:
8%

White:
66%

International:
5%

Unknown:
0%

Out of State:
75%

Political Activity

Columbia tends to be a liberal campus, although there are pockets of conservative strongholds that thrive as well. Because of the history of the last few years, in New York and internationally, Columbia kids have gotten more involved and outspoken concerning their beliefs and opinions, all of which are visible on the opinion page of The Spectator every day

Gay Tolerance

Columbia is a fairly liberal school in a very diverse city, so there aren't many problems with gay tolerance.

Economic Status

A lot of Columbia kids come from privileged backgrounds, but there's also a large number of students on financial aid, from different countries and walks of life.

Most Popular Religions:

Judaism and Christianity.

Minority Clubs

The following give an idea of the minority clubs at Columbia, but there are many, many, more (see the list of student organizations at the back of the book):

- Taiwanese American Students Association (TASA) Thai Student Association
- Queers of Color
- Romanian Society
- Russian International
- Association of Columbia

- Korean Students Association (KSA)
- Latino Heritage Month
- Liga Filipina
- Grupo Quisqueyano (GQ)
- Haitian Students Association

Students Speak Out On...
Diversity

> "I feel like I am in Wonder Breadville. However, I heard from others that this is the most diverse Ivy league school that you will ever find. It is not diverse enough in comparison to the city in which it is located."

Q "With hundreds of clubs and activities, Columbia has something for everyone from debate to fencing. Columbia attracts students from all over the globe. **There are no dominant ethnic groups**, be they Caucasian, Asian, or other. The common denominator here is achievement – not race, culture, religion or social class."

Q "**Extremely diverse** - it's NYC, after all."

Q "I'd say the campus is extremely diverse. There are **tons of minorities on campus,** with the largest groups being Jewish students and Asians."

Q "There are **over one hundred countries represented** in the student body. No matter what language you speak or want to speak I would venture so far as to say that you will never have any problem finding an interlocutor."

Q "Columbia **prides itself on diversity.** That said, there isn't much racial mixing."

Q "It's incredibly diverse. **You meet people from all walks of life** here."

Q "It is the **most diverse Ivy League** university."

Q "Columbia is **the most diverse of the Ivies;** that's why I chose to come here. I've met people of all types and personalities, and it's been an awesome experience from my sheltered, Catholic school background."

Q "It's New York! **You can find anyone of any nationality** here; it's great!"

Q "There are **many diverse things going on** from theatrical, to political, to religious, to musical events—anything. It's a great place."

Q "I have met a lot of really **amazing individuals** who are so smart, unique, musical, athletic or funny—all the while being really normal, which is a huge plus! I was somewhat worried about the Ivy stereotype of super dweebs and ridiculously rich kids. Granted there are a few of those, but everyone at Columbia is just really grounded and normal and fun! The City, well, what can be said? It's amazing! It is still, by far, the best place on earth, and sometimes my friends and I literally stop and say, 'My god, we live here!' There's just so much to see and do and be; it never ends!"

Q "The last time I checked, Columbia was something like third nationally with respect to foreign students. **There are a lot of Jews like myself**, and there also a lot of Asians. Columbia is very diverse, and it is all for the best!"

Q "It's very diverse; but **we could use more diversity of character instead of ethnicity.**"

Q "I think that Columbia is the most diverse school in the Ivy League, and **it's apparent from the very first second you step on campus.** The only thing about Columbia is that sometimes people tend to get into cliques, but if you're open to making all sorts of friends then it won't be a problem."

$\mathcal{Q}$ "I personally feel like **I have a very diverse group of friends**, however, at the same time, I feel that many of the minority groups can be very cliquish. Though there are large numbers of minorities on campus, there is not always that much interaction between the different groups."

The College Prowler Take On...
Diversity

As far as Ivy League colleges go, Columbia boasts that it is by far the most diverse. Many languages are spoken across campus and most cultural or religious groups have clubs or organizations to preserve and celebrate their identity. Despite representing many countries and ethnicities, Columbia still remains a college of the caucasian persuasion.

Columbia succeeds in being diverse, but interestingly, the desire to succeed is a value that transcends race, nationality and class. The school is located in New York City, which offers more diversity than probably any other location in the United States. With over eight million people and hundreds of languages spoken, finding a people, a culture or a lifestyle is not far away.

A-

The College Prowler™ Grade on
Diversity: A-

A high grade in Diversity indicates that ethnic minorities and international students have a notable presence on campus and that students of different economic backgrounds, religious beliefs, and sexual preferences are well-represented.

Guys & Girls

The Lowdown On...
Guys & Girls

Men Undergrads:
53%

Women Undergrads:
47%

Birth Control Available?
Yes, at the health services office.

Social Scene:
Drinking is what people do at Columbia, if they have any social life at all. Most bars in the area draw a specific crowd, so you have a pretty good idea of who you'll see based on where you go before you even get there. But the bonus about going to school in New York is when you tire of area bars (or if you never wanted to drink in the first place), there's a whole city out there to explore and entertain yourself with.

Hookups or Relationships?

Like most colleges these days, Columbia isn't a place where people date. Serious relationships are not an anomaly, but few claim to have met the love of their life at CU. Hookups happen, although some might claim that some of the nerdier students are too gunshy to be as free-lovin' as kids at other schools.

Best Place to Meet Guys/Girls:

Your friends and lovers will come mostly from your participation in extracurricular activities, whether it's debate or drama.

Dress Code

Columbia's got room for all kinds—the indie rockers, the label whores, even the Abercrombie lovers have their support at Columbia. You can wear what you want, but for the most part, it's a laid-back jeans kinda place.

Did You Know?

Top Places to Find Hotties:
1. The library
2. The Hungarian Pastry Shop
3. The bar

Top Places to Hookup:
1. In the stacks of Butler library
2. Your tiny single dorm room
3. At the bar

Students Speak Out On...
Guys & Girls

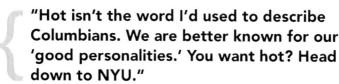

{ **"Hot isn't the word I'd used to describe Columbians. We are better known for our 'good personalities.' You want hot? Head down to NYU."**

Q "The guys are bookish for the most part and **the girls are conservative and very buttoned-up.** I often have a hard time understanding what some of them are doing in a raging city like New York but I guess that's just one more aspect of the city's diversity. If you're looking for hotties you've got to go and hang out down in Soho."

Q "Both the men and women of Columbia tend to fall into one of two categories regarding personal style: **fashionistas or it-looks/smells-ok-so-I'll-just-wear-my-jeans mode.** Each type is easy to spot. Men tend to wear more hair products than the women do and it is rare to find girls who wear a lot of makeup. Low maintenance appearance seems to rule the day."

Q "The **dating scene here is strange.** People don't really date. They just hang out as friends and maybe a relationship develops, but that is rare. There is an abundance of happily single people at Columbia."

Q "The **good-looking ones are in short supply**, but the good news is that there are many who are very smart and very willing."

Q "If it's stereotypical hotties you seek, then **check out the gym.** They tend to migrate there in order to admire their own beauty."

Q "Though it didn't stop me from trying and failing, the **women at Columbia have big egos and it's a huge turnoff.** Everything is always about them and it gets old after a while. Hot is a matter of opinion, it's better than high school I'll say. I think the men aren't so great but I'm not interested in them so what do I know."

Q "**There are definitely hot boys on campus** and in New York in general. Everyone is really laidback. It's definitely not a school where you feel you have to have a significant other."

Q "Columbia is **nerdy but hot.**"

Q "Columbia's not known for its good-looking people, but it **gets better every year!** I find that since there are so few really hot guys, the ones that are hot are complete jerks. I know this from plenty of experience with the type. Oh, and for hot girls, guys generally seek the company of Barnard."

Q "**I wouldn't know.** I didn't go to school to check out people."

Q "New York City, in general, has **a lot of gays and lesbians.** It is New York City—it's diverse and it's a big school with a zillion clubs and organizations. I think anyone can find their niche if they look for it."

Q "You can find anyone you want here. **I personally love the hot grad students** who wait tables at the local cafes!"

Q "**You never appreciate what you have.** The guys think the girls are hotter at other schools, and the girls think the guys are hotter at other schools. The guys from other schools think our girls are hot and the girls from other schools … well, you get the picture. Overall, there's a decent looking bunch on both ends."

Q "I have no idea what the guys are like; I don't swing that way, but **the girls are hot!**

Q "Well, as a Columbia guy, I have to say that coming to Columbia might not be the best thing for a woman. Because Barnard (an all-girls college) is right across the street, **guys are outnumbered.** I don't have a problem with this ratio, but my female friends often do."

Q "The student body **leaves something to be desired.** The average Columbia kid is a wealthy, self-important, bright person. The guys are generally bad at hitting on girls. The girls usually are immature and naive. It's a very liberal campus, and a lot of the students take stands and stage minor protests about ridiculous causes. Sometimes it's amusing."

Q "Personally, I think **there's a lot of eye candy.**"

Q "I really don't think there are that many attractive girls on campus. **A lot of guys tend to date girls from Barnard.** Between Barnard and Columbia, there are many more girls than guys; Columbia girls kind of resent Barnard because of this. I don't think that most guys on campus would be considered good-looking either. Overall, I feel like most of the smart schools I've been to have people who are never that good looking."

Q "We're not known for hot guys; **we're known for smart ones.**"

Q **"Hot girls? No, not too many of them.** I managed to meet some hot girls in my four years, though."

Q "Socially, you get people who think they're the ultimate mix of being smart and cool. **They leave a lot to be desired in both cases**. The incoming classes seem to be getting better and better looking. My class was pretty, but the recent incoming freshmen were really good-looking."

Q "I have no idea what the guys are like; I don't swing that way, but **the girls are hot!**

Q "There are some decent guys, but **there isn't an abundance of hotties at all.** In general, you can find some good people at Columbia; it's just a matter of luck and patience."

The College Prowler Take On...
Guys & Girls

Although most students believe that Columbia is not the place to find lots of hotties, they seem to agree that both the men and women who attend are rather attractive. The place on campus to spot the certifiable hotties is the gym, but people also seem to find visual fulfillment at the local bars around campus or down in Soho. It is not unheard of to have some lookers in class too. There is, of course, all of New York City to ogle.

Many students say that they came to Columbia to study, not to focus on romance, and they are unfazed by the school's reputed lack of eye candy. That said, the students are usually ambitious and interesting, so sometimes mental attraction is more possible and even sought after. Likewise, there's plenty of hooking up going on at Columbia and serious relationships as well. If you seek it, you can probably find it. There are all types here, from the high-maintenance princesses to the shower-and-wear-jeans crowd. There are always some great looking people around campus. You just have to keep your eyes open for whoever melts your butter.

The College Prowler™ Grade on
Guys: B-

A high grade for Guys indicates that the male population on campus is attractive, smart, friendly, and engaging, and that the school has a decent ratio of guys to girls.

The College Prowler™ Grade on
Girls: C+

A high grade for Girls not only implies that the women on campus are attractive, smart, friendly, and engaging, but also that there is a fair ratio of girls to guys.

Athletics

The Lowdown On...
Athletics

Athletic Division:
Division I

Conference:
Ivy League

**Male Undergraduate
Varsity Athletes:**
419 (4%)

**Female Undergraduate
Varsity Athletes:**
336 (3%)

School Mascot:
Lion

Colors:
Scarlet and White

➜

Men's Varsity Teams:
Baseball
Basketball
Cross-country
Fencing
Field hockey
Football
Golf
Soccer
Swimming and diving
Tennis
Track and field (indoor)
Track and field (outdoor)
Wrestling

Women's Varsity Teams:
Archery
Basketball
Cross-country
Fencing
Lacrosse
Soccer
Softball
Swimming and diving
Tennis
Track and field (indoor)
Track and field (outdoor)
Volleyball
Rowing

Club Sports:
Aikido
Archery
Armed and unarmed self-defenes
Ballroom and latin dance team
Boxing
Cricket
Cycling
Equestrian
Figure skaitng
Hiking
Hockey
Judo
Kayak
Lacrosse
Masters swim
Road runners
Rugby
Sailing
Shotokan karate
Skiing
Squash
Swimming
Table tennis
Ultimate frisbee
Volleyball
Water polo
Wing chun kung fu.

Getting Tickets

Students get in free to sporting events at Columbia, but they're not very popular, so getting in is never a problem. .

Most Popular Sports

The football and basketball teams are most discussed at Columbia, the latter having gotten a new coach last year.

Overlooked Teams:

Most often, the women's teams are stronger than the men's (most notably the crew team) and generally don't get enough recognition for that.

Best Place to Take a Walk

Riverside Park and Central Park.

Athletic Fields:

Baker Field.

Gyms/Facilities

Marcellus Hartley Dodge Fitness Center

The fitness center offers an indoor track, a wide array of cardio and weight machines, aerobics rooms where yoga and dance classes are held and locker rooms with showers and saunas. During the week, it's open from 6:15 a.m. to midnight, which gives everyone pretty much no excuse to skip working out.

Levien Gymnasium

The gym is huge, filled with bleachers and offers a great place to play basketball when varsity teams aren't in there practicing.

Uris Pool

The pool is huge and everybody uses it, especially you when you have to take your swim test in order to graduate.

Students Speak Out On...
Athletics

"Unfortunately sports—of any kind—do not play a major role in undergraduate life unless you are a participant."

Q "**Embarrassing** - but they try so hard."

Q "Many people are surprised to learn that Columbia even has football, basketball, baseball and soccer teams. They are there for those who enjoy watching and competing in collegiate sports, but **not many people attend these events.** This is due in part to the fact that the fields and stadiums are nowhere near campus and the activities are not widely publicized."

Q "There are many athletic opportunities at Columbia, but they are usually **not as popular as they are at other schools.**"

Q "We have **sports at Columbia?**"

Q "**Nobody cares about sports** and I sometimes wish people did because then the teams might do a little better. Columbia varsity sports are usually a joke. IM sports are little better, rugby and disc are popular."

The College Prowler Take On...
Athletics

Some students are surprised to learn that Columbia has sports teams at all. Athletics are not a priority on campus, except for those who participate in them. Columbia is known for its academics, not its athletics, and many non-athletes (that is, most Columbians) rip on campus athletics any chance they can get. If you asked an engineering student if he went to last week's football game, he would likely look at you as if you were deranged. Perhaps if Baker Field were not one hundred blocks north of Columbia's main campus, students would be more inclined to support Columbia's athletes.

There are plenty of sporting opportunities available to those wishing to participate or watch such as rugby, intramural soccer and other sports. When the weather is good, it's likely to see people participating in all sorts of athletics on the lawns in front of Butler Library. Crew and fencing are popular sports on campus. Those interested in athletics should check out the Spectator (Columbia's primary student newspaper) to learn more about our Lions.

The College Prowler™ Grade on

Athletics: F

A high grade in Athletics indicates that students have school spirit, that sports programs are respected, that games are well-attended, and that intramurals are a prominent part of student life.

Nightlife

The Lowdown On...
Nightlife

Popular Nightlife Spots!

Club Crawler:

There are no clubs in the area immediately surrounding Columbia, but if you head downtown, there is a huge scene of all-night places (frequented more by NYU students than anyone from Columbia). If you're not into ecstasy, you may want to skip the club scene altogether.

Cream

246 Columbus Ave

(212) 633-9800

This Upper West Side bar & club is more laidback than the haute culture of the rest of the club scene in Manhattan, and offers a fun, casual locale for shaking of groove things.

Etoile

109 E 56th St

(212) 750-5656

Another swankfest, Etoile is connected to the Lombardy Hotel and serves the bold and the beautiful.

➜

Float

240 West 52nd Street

(212) 581-0055

Dance the night away with the ultrahip divas of Manhattan—if you're beautiful and rich enough to make it past the door, the world is yours. Don't expect to make it to the private party rooms upstairs though, they're reserved for Ashanti and other VIPs.

Bar Prowler:
1020

1020 Amsterdam Avenue

(212) 531-3468

1020 is the favorite among upperclassmen and some graduate students. The pool table in the back also draws neighborhood folk who just want to shoot a few rounds and drink a few pints. A big screen in the back plays the big game or often whatever movie is on TBS or AMC.

The Abbey Pub

237 West 105th St.

(212) 222-8713

The ten block walk to the Abbey can be hard to handle on a very cold night, but the table service and friendly, laid-back atmosphere can be worth it. The Abbey Pub used to be known for serving alcohol to anyone, including those entering the bar in strollers, but recent crackdowns have changed the rules. They're still a bit soft on the Ids though.

Cannon's

2794 Broadway

(212) 678-9738

A favorite among Columbia athletes, Cannon's has pitcher specials most nights of the week and a rowdy, fun attitude. For the strong-hearted.

Ding Dong

929 Columbus Avenue

(212) 663-2600

The indie-rock undergrads at Columbia rejoiced when this dingy, punk-rock dive bar moved to town last year. But all drinkers agree, the Ding Dong is an unpretentious place to drink cheap and listen to something other than pop radio (live DJs mosts of the week help keep the music interesting).

The Heights

2867 Broadway

(212) 866-7035

Half-price margaritas during Happy hours—5-7 and again from 11-12—make this a great place, though it's quite small, so don't expect room to breathe. A great place to drink when the roof is open, offering more air and a slice of the New York skyline.

Nacho Mama's

2893 Broadway

(212) 665-2800

A favorite amongst sorority girls and male athletes, Nacho's is usually a pretty safe bet for eye candy (which, granted, are sometimes way-too-drunk freshmen girls) and they have a late night happy hour—half price drinks from 11 to midnight. Look your best and act your nicest, though, as the bouncers can be quite stringent and make you wait outside (which all Columbians agree is a little strange in the un-swanky neighborhood of Morningside Heights).

Night Café

938 Amsterdam Avenue

(212) 864-8889

The dive bar to end all dive bars, the clientele at Night Café looks like a lineup at the local precinct. But sometimes you want to drink in a place where the music blares sad, drinkin' tunes and cocaine isn't too hard to find in the men's bathroom.

SoHa

988 Amsterdam Avenue

(212) 678-0098

Known in the neighborhood as "the bar where girls dance on the tables," SoHa is a great local place to shake your groove thing with like-minded fun-seekers. There is a dress code, but it's basically no sneakers. Go in your New York Suit of Black and you'll be fine.

The West End

2911 Broadway

(212) 662-8830

There's hardly anything you can say about a bar whose slogan is "Where Columbia had its first beer," except that everybody goes there. It's the closest bar to the main gates of campus and most residence halls so everyone is familiar with it, making it a popular place to assemble for a study lunch (which can slide slowly into a non-study happy hour, as the draft pints are practically free from 4-7 every day) or a night out. Fortunately, the place is as big as a barn, so there's room for all who are thirsty and a lounge in the basement is often a spot for local and campus bands to play.

Bars Close At:

4 a.m.

Other Places to Check Out

The closest non-Columbia bars are on the Upper West Side, mainly between 80th and 90th on Amsterdam (and a few on Columbus). Bourbon Street gets a fair number of Columbians trickling south (Amsterdam and 82nd), but for a nice change of pace, try the Dublin House on 79th between Broadway and Amsterdam. It's a lowkey watering hole whose bartenders are all Irish. If you want more swanky or high-class, try the Evelyn Lounge on Columbus at 79th Street. The drinks are pricey, but so are the people. There are loads more in the area and all over Manhattan (Brooklyn, too, if you like riding the subway all night long); just pick up a Zagat's guide to nightlife and put on your drinkin' shoes.

Primary Areas with Nightlife

Morningside Heights has a number of campus bars, but all of New York has booze and nighttime fun aplenty to offer.

Cheapest Place to Get a Drink

Unless it's happy hour, plan on paying four or five bucks for a pint just about anywhere you go, except of course, upscale places, where cocktails can run from six or seven dollars all the way to fifteen.

Local Specialties

Because most drinking goes on in bars, the special drink is whatever the hell you want—the bartenders are well-trained, their bars are completely stocked. Settle down with a G&T if you want, but don't hesitate to ask for a dry martini, a Sammy Smith's oatmeal stout, or even a blue whale. Well, maybe you guys should hesitate on that last one.

Favorite Drinking Games

Beer Pong and Beirut have been known to occur at frat houses, but most Columbia students prefer not to engage in the tomfoolery of drinking games. They just go ahead and drink.

What to Do if You're Not 21

The great thing about going to college in New York is that if your idea of fun doesn't involve shooting kamikazes or even sipping a Guinness, there's loads of other stuff to do—Caroline's (1626 Broadway, (212) 757-4100) is a great comedy club at Times Square that books class acts, there's Amsterdam Billiards (344 Amsterdam Avenue, (212) 496-8180) on the Upper West Side and, and Drip (489 Amsterdam Ave, (212) 875-1032) is a great coffee shop where singles hang out and eye each other, even on Saturday night.

Organization Parties

Every year, ADP, the gay and lesbian fraternity-organization, sponsors Hot Jazz, a semi-formal with live jazz and free champagne (for the $30 price of admission). Not to be missed.

People who live in spaces that are big enough to hold others have parties from time to time. They can be really fun (Woodbridge parties tend to worth the iwndy walk towards the river) and sometimes not—it gets very hot in the East Campus duplexes, although you can always escape to the roof for some air. But with a few cheap handles and a good theme, any meager Columbia dorm can turn into a worthwhile Saturday night, and generally, parties remain unbothered by security.

Frats

See the Greek Section!

Students Speak Out On...
Nightlife

"Parties in the Columbia-owned apartments are different. Since there are no security guards in most of these buildings the celebrations can get pretty wild."

Q "Most on-campus parties (frats, service groups) suck, **you can't help but feel lame** at them. The bar scene is...a college bar scene I guess, and where you fit in depends on your level of self respect and what you want to get out of drinking."

Q "Feeling like a dive? Go to The West End, or The Heights. Want the downtown feel uptown? Go to Sip, or SoHa. There is a bar or club on every block in the Village, and the bonus is you get to interact with NYU hotties. **Go to Soho if you need a celebrity fix.**"

Q "There's **something for everyone in New York**. Columbia is not known for its party scene which is quite frankly pretty low key. Venturing out into the city always promises a new adventure. There are great dives and bumping clubs in every neighborhood from Williamsburg and Brooklyn to the Lower East Side and Chelsea. Winsomeness will get you a long way."

Q "The **school-sponsored parties including barbecues and picnics are almost always fun**, provided that they do not run out of food. Each college of Columbia has special events geared to their students such as casino nights, career dinners and cocktail parties. Many students attend the school-run events and for the most part, they enjoy themselves."

Q "I did not go to many parties or bars. **I am paying outrageous tutition here so how can I waste my time like that?**"

Q "**Some parties suck** because there are a few kegs of cheap beer, but there is not even a bag of chips to share, so you have lots of hungry drunken students. Not a good combination. A word to the wise – have a snack before you go to a party unless you know the host supplies grub for their guests."

The College Prowler Take On...
Nightlife

Comb the world over and it is impossible to find a place with as happening a nightlife as New York. There are enough restaurants, cafes, clubs, museums, galleries, exotic movie houses, theater and sporting events to keep anyone occupied. The Morningside Heights neighborhood alone has bars and hang-outs aplenty to fill the desires of the majority of the student population. Private student parties can be fun as well, provided that the people are interesting. The various schools at Columbia schedule many events for their students that are designed to allow the people to mingle. The West End and other local bars are packed during academic down times. Some live for gala type openings at clubs and restaurants, but you should make sure you are on "the list" before attempting to crash these venues.

The weekend officially begins on Thursdays around Columbia and the bars can be busy. As fun as the city can be, it is very expensive and tiring—bars are open till 4 a.m. and many clubs stay open later. Some prefer the local scene just because it can be less costly than going downtown. Others live on Top Ramen for a week to be able to have one night out in the city, but they would probably agree that it was worth the sacrifice.

The College Prowler™ Grade on

Nightlife: A

A high grade in Nightlife indicates that there are many bars and clubs in the area that are easily accessible and affordable. Other determining factors include the number of options for the under-21 crowd and the prevalence of house parties.

Greek Life

The Lowdown On...
Greek Life

Number of Fraternities:
15

Number of Sororities:
12

Undergrad Men in Fraternities:
15%

Undergrad Women in Sororities:
9%

Fraternities on Campus:
Alpha Epsilon Pi
Delta Sigma Phi
Kappa Delta Rho
Phi Epsilon Pi
Phi Iota Alpha
Lambda Phi Epsilon
Pi Kappa Alpha
Sigma Chi
Sigma Nu
Sigma Phi Epsilon
Zeta Psi

→

Sororities on Campus:

Alpha Chi Omega
Alpha Kappa Alpha
Delta Gamma
Kappa Alpha Theta
Delta Sigma Theta
Lambda Pi Chi
Sigma Delta Tau

Other Greek Organizations:

Greek Council
Greek Peer Advisors
Interfraternity Council
Order of Omega
Panhellenic Council
Intergreek Council.

Multicultural Colonies:

Alpha Delta Phi

Did You Know?

Columbia has a chapter of St. Anthony's Hall, a semi-secret literary society that has only a few chapters at elite schools in the U.S. While they're known at other schools as being snobby intellectuals, their reputation at Columbia is only as snobs. Typically, they're among the wealthiest students at Columbia. But before you turn up your nose, remember, they throw parties with open bars every Thursday night at their beautiful brownstone on 116th and Riverside Drive, so best to befriend them if you can.

Students Speak Out On...
Greek Life

> "Don't come to Columbia expecting to go to big-time frat parties every night or anything like that. Most of the social life at Columbia is found outside of campus in the city."

Q "Frats and sororities are around campus, but **they definitely don't dominate the social scene.** The thing about the social life around campus is that, because we're in the biggest city in the world, people spend a lot of time exploring New York and less time around campus."

Q "Greek life exists—**quietly.**"

Q "Greek life at Columbia is **pretty lame.**"

Q "The **frats and sororities are jokes,** as are their members. Who the hell pays to associate with a group of frat "friends" when you have all of New York to explore? What defect of imagination causes this?"

Q "Greek life is **present but small** at Columbia."

Q "Fortunately, **Greek life does not dominate the social scene.** When we first got there, everyone thought it was pretty lame. I have no idea what the sororities are ... except for Theta—supposedly, that's the one for all the hottest (and easiest) chicks on campus. But anyway, I think Greek life is lame. There are tons of frat parties and events, but it's definitely not the focus of social life. Come to think of it, I guess they do have some pretty cool events, like AmJam—it's just utter and total debauchery."

Q "Believe it or not, I actually rushed a sorority first semester. Unfortunately, I didn't decide to go through with the pledging process. **Greek life is not big at all** on campus. There's really no presence."

Q "**It's there if you want it,** but it definitely does not dominate the social scene."

Q "It **doesn't really dominate unless you want to.** However, I think that there were record amounts girls who rushed for sororities this year."

Q "There is a Greek row down one of the side streets with all the frat and sorority houses. **I don't see how it could be that big, though**; it is New York City."

Q "I am not too sure about Greek life, but **if it's your bag then go for it.** I will probably rush second semester, once I get a feel for life on campus. But, if I find that sorority life isn't for me, then I will continue to live in the dorms."

Q "Greek life **definitely does not dominate,** but it is around. Once in awhile, they have some great events. We are actually known for only having such a small percentage of our students in frats and sororities, but they are totally there and available for your enjoyment, pledge, free alcohol, and somewhat-cool dudes."

Q "Greek life is small. **I was in a fraternity, and I liked it.** It doesn't dominate the scene, but it is fun for those who are in it. I'd check it out and see what you think."

Q "**Greeks are among the more social people,** but the scene is not dominated by them. Many of the frats, like my own, are associated with a sports team (for example, Sigma Nu = swimmers, Sigma Chi = football players, Kappa Delta Rho = basketball players). There are only four sororities. My favorite among them is Kappa Alpha Theta; a lot of them are really cute and fun girls."

Q "Greek life does not dominate. **You make what you want of it.** If you want to be part of a sorority that is up to you, but it's not like if you're not in one you won't meet people."

Q "Greek life is **not that big of a deal.** I'd say that only a really small percent of students are probably involved in it. When there are so many great bars and clubs in the city, frat parties tend to lose their appeal."

Q "There are a few fraternity parties each year, but **they are packed and the bad beer keeps flowing**, so it's worth going to at least one to check it out."

Q "Greek life is a **complete joke at Columbia.** Fraternities and sororities definitely do not have the same meaning and clout that they do at other universities. Houses that try to act like those at state universities get laughed at."

The College Prowler Take On...
Greek Life

Students agree that there is not much of a Greek Life at Columbia. While there are fraternities and sororities, they do not dominate the social scene. Those involved in the Greek system, however, seem to really enjoy it. Perhaps because there is so much going on at Columbia in the way of academics and extracurricular activities and with the whole city of New York as a playground, the Greek life does not have much to add on this campus. Since you don't have to be in a frat or go to a frat to drink beer and meet people, most Columbia students choose not to.

The Greek system does exist at Columbia, but it's very self-contained. It's not the kind of school where people think you're cool if you made it into Pi Kappa Alpha and most Columbia kids couldn't name more than one fraternity or sorority, if they could even name one. The Greek system is also tied closely to the athletic world—athletes are Greek and the Greek are athletes. Like all groups at Columbia, the Greeks enjoy their way-of-life, it just happens not to be the center of attention at CU.

The College Prowler™ Grade on

Greek Life: C-

A high grade in Greek Life indicates that sororities and fraternities are not only present, but also active on campus. Other determining factors include the variety of houses available and the respect the Greek community receives from the rest of the campus.

Drug Scene

The Lowdown On...
Drug Scene

Most Prevalent Drugs on Campus:
Alcohol
Marijuana

Liquor-Related Referrals:
31

Liquor-Related Arrests:
0

Drug-Related Referrals:
22

Drug-Related Arrests:
0

Drug Counseling Programs:

Health services offers smoking cessation seminars, which meet weekly for eight weeks each semester and discuss relaxation techniques, behavioral condition, and medication options.

In addition to Counseling and Psychological Services, Nightline (x7777), a student-run all-night phone line, provides an outlet for students who need a safe and anonymous person to talk to.

Students Speak Out On...
Drug Scene

"People smoke up. I guess some do harder drugs. If you don't want to, there are plenty of people who don't."

Q "**Marijuana is the illegal drug of choice** and it is almost always available and it's tough not to be exposed to a possible contact high at most parties. There's very little peer pressure concerning having a nonuser join in. The potheads would rather keep their stash than waste it on someone who does not even want to try it. This drug is highly visible in the social scene, but it is the individual's choice on whether or not to partake in this vice."

Q "**Alcohol, nicotine and caffeine** are the drugs of choice on campus and they are in great abundance."

Q "I don't know. I presume there are people who do use, but then again, a lot don't. **Drinking is quite prevalent**, though."

Q "**Lots of uppers**, especially in the scientific realm."

Q "Word has it that study **drugs like ritalin and cocaine dominate the scene during exam periods**, but I have yet to see anything of the sort. Caffeine seems to be the drug of choice as all of the coffee shops and tea houses tend to be overcrowded all semester long. Columbia comes off as being a very serious place."

Q "**Drugs are very popular.** But many people I know, myself included, swore off drugs by the end of the year. They get old and the serious abusers are such dicks that I want nothing in common with them."

Q "**Lots of people do drugs**, but some don't."

Q "I don't think the drug scene is that prevalent, but **if you want drugs, you can definitely get them.** I don't think there's that much hard drug usage. Mostly, it's weed and ecstasy."

Q "**If you're into it, you'll know about it;** if you're not, then you won't. There's no pressure to do anything you don't want to do, and you don't have to worry about being tricked into taking something. Almost everybody drinks; it could be a problem if you're a recovering alcoholic."

Q "As far as drugs go ... **all I know of is alcohol.**"

Q "It is New York City. If you want drugs, you shall find them. **Finding a dealer is pretty easy.**"

Q "If you want them **you'll find them**."

Q "There are drugs on campus but **not in abundance.** At Columbia, they are something that can be easily avoided, that's for sure. There's never a pressure; either you smoke pot or you don't, and people are really cool with that, thankfully. Pot is the biggest drug on campus, though I am sure there are other things floating around."

Q "It's college. **There's lots of pot,** and coke is pretty popular, too. Ecstasy seems to be a bit slower making a splash on the scene, but it's there and getting bigger. Basically, if you want to be in the scene, you won't have a problem, and if you don't, you may not even realize it's there."

Q "**Drugs are available if you want them,** but they're not required to have a good time."

Q "**I really didn't see much of the drug scene** since the crowd I hung with was more into alcohol than anything else, but I hear it's around. I don't know much about it though, other than that there are numerous pot-smokers."

The College Prowler Take On...
Drug Scene

Consensus among students regarding drugs is that if you want them, you can get them. Caffeine is the drug of choice, but alcohol, nicotine, and marijuana are not far behind. Harder drugs are not unheard of and very possible to attain, but they are not as visible and unless you're sniffing them out, you'd never know cocaine, ecstasy, or acid were present. Study drugs are rumored to thrive in certain disciplines. Use and abuse of alcohol and marijuana runs rampant on weekends or during slow periods, but because of the dedication of the majority of the student body, few students are willing to risk their academic future by partying too hard during the school week.

For those who do not wish to imbibe or get stoned, you do not have to be exposed to those things if you choose your friends wisely, however, it is commonplace to see the squarest of students guzzling vodka and/or sharing a joint at a party. Despite the fact that many students cut loose with some kind of substance, nobody will mock you if you opt out. Columbia is chock full of very hard-working ambitious kids who would choose a good night's sleep over seven Kamikazes and a hangover that won't allow any reading to get done the next day.

B-

The College Prowler™ Grade on

Drug Scene: B-

A high grade in the Drug Scene indicates that drugs are not a noticeable part of campus life; drug use is not visible, and no pressure to use them seems to exist.

Campus
Strictness

The Lowdown On...
Campus Strictness

What Are You Most Likely to Get Caught Doing on Campus?

• Drinking from an open container

Students Speak Out On...
Campus Strictness

"Campus police is a rather non-intrusive entity in campus life. That's not to say that they tolerate drug use but they by no means pry into the lives of the students."

Q "Depends on your RA and how out of control you get. Most students who get busted get second chances, and security is more concerned with keeping you safe and healthy than enforcing law (i.e. calling an ambulance if you get alcohol poisoning instead of the cops)."

Q "There is **always someone willing to buy alcohol for a youngin'** who wants to drink in his room. Don't get caught with an open container on campus (even if you are legal); it's not appreciated by campus security, and you may be put on report. As long as campus security cannot see alcohol or drug use then you are ok. If you are caught, especially with illegal substances, your tenure at Columbia may be revoked."

Q "I'd say the **campus police are pretty lax about drugs and drinking and stuff.** When dorm parties get busted, no one ever really gets in trouble. The worst thing that will happen is that the people who live in the suite throwing the party might get probation, so they can't throw another party for the rest of the semester ... but even that's rare. A lot of it depends on your RA. Some RAs are stricter than others about drinking and drugs. However, I think it's mainly the freshman RAs that are strict."

Q "I **haven't been caught.**"

Q "**They leave you alone** unless you're obvious."

Q "They give you a warning if you get into huge trouble. Resident assistants **(RAs) are usually pretty cool.** You just need to be discreet about breaking the rules."

Q "Ummm ... there's this group called CAVA in case of emergencies. They came to your room and rush you to the hospital if there is any kind of dangerous drug or alcohol situation. **Columbia is a pretty wet campus,** I'd say. But, as long as you drink discreetly, there should be no problems."

Q "I haven't had a problem. **Many smoke pot on campus right in the open.**"

Q "Mostly RAs and building people deal with stuff like drugs and drinking. When there is a huge problem, campus police will get called. **No one is too strict; you get away with a lot.**"

Q "The first week I was on campus, **I literally sat out on the quad and smoked weed with friends.** I also threw a keg party in my suite, although kegs aren't allowed in the dorms. I wouldn't be worried at all, especially once you get your fake ID, which you should get as soon as you get into the City."

Q "**I don't think that the police handle much of the things related to drugs and drinking.** Your RAs look after you, but I'm not into that stuff. If those things bother you, you can report it to your RA or someone higher and try to get the problem resolved."

Q "**No one cares too much about drinking or anything.** You can generally smoke pot in peace. If you want to do ecstasy, then you'll probably be at a club, and no one will know. If you want to do coke, like many rich kids, then you are an idiot!"

The College Prowler Take On...
Campus Strictness

Students agree that campus security is willing to look the other way concerning first time alcohol and marijuana offenses. Within the dorms, the RAs have the power to enforce drug and underage drinking policies, but most do not. If you get caught, expulsion is a possibility.

Since most alcohol and drug use is limited to the rooms or apartments, it is less likely that students will get caught. There is a big difference between four people drinking in a dorm room and a wild kegger, and the latter tends to be hard to achieve in Columbia's tiny dorm rooms and apartments. If you are not obviously intoxicated, then you can get away with just about anything. If you live in a dorm and are too drunk to hand the security guard your ID yourself (i.e. your friend does), the guard is required to call CAVA (the student-run emergency care group). It's always health over legality at CU, and an underage drunk student who is taken to the hospital will rarely face disciplinary actions. Use discretion. While security is rather lenient, the safety of students is a priority.

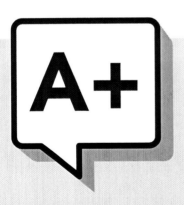

The College Prowler™ Grade on

Campus Strictness: A+

A high Campus Strictness grade implies an overall lenient atmosphere; police and RAs are fairly tolerant, and the administration's rules are flexible.

Parking

The Lowdown On...
Parking

CU Parking Services
Absolutely none

Student Parking Lot?
No

Freshman Allowed to Park?
No

Did You Know?

Best Places to Find a Parking Spot

New Jersey

Good Luck Getting a Parking Spot Here!

Manhattan

Parking Permits

There are none. You can get a spot in a garage for a couple hundred bucks a month.

Students Speak Out On...
Parking

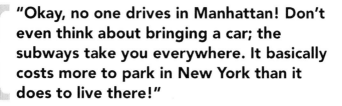

"Okay, no one drives in Manhattan! Don't even think about bringing a car; the subways take you everywhere. It basically costs more to park in New York than it does to live there!"

Q "Don't bring a car. There is no parking and lots cost upwards of $200 per month. Former car owners may temporarily suffer from car envy – that is until they hear **horror stories of people taking two hours to find a parking spot** that happens to be 10 blocks away from their destination. That situation is not fun and it serves as a reminder that cars are not a necessity in New York."

Q "**Parking?** There's parking on campus???"

Q "Parking is all but **impossible**. This is New York. There's no need to have a car."

Q "Parking is **not an option.** Columbia is in the city. Parking spaces are about $300 per month, so no one has a car."

Q "Ha-ha ... **Don't bring a car.** Parking in that neighborhood is a pain. You don't need a car; everyone takes the subway."

Q "**Parking in New York City?** Ha!"

Q "You really **can't have a car at Columbia**, and they're completely unnecessary."

Q "I commute to Columbia. **It's really hard to find parking unless you get monthly parking at a garage**; but for that, you need to sign up months in advance. Otherwise, you can find parking on the street if you come in early enough."

Q "**You don't need a car**, just a Metrocard."

Q "No. **Don't bring a car.** Bad idea."

Q "It's **pretty impossible** to have a car in the first place. The subway, buses, and cabs are the best way to go. Living in New York City really makes you appreciate the convenience of public transportation."

Q "There is **no parking scene on campus.** There's only really expensive parking garages and street parking, which can be pretty hard to get. I don't know a single student who owns a car in the City. Even most professors ride the subway or find some other form of transportation."

The College Prowler Take On...
Parking

Don't bring a car. There is no parking on campus and local garages are very expensive. Those used to owning a car might find the inability to drive to be off-putting, but after a while, it is a blessing. There is very little street parking near campus, so those who do drive to school often have to park upwards of 20 blocks away.

It is not worth the heartache or expense to bring a car to Columbia. Bringing a car to Columbia is like taking your mom on a first date. It's a nice idea but the reality could be disastrous. When you need a car fix, take a cab or daydream about being able to afford a driver.

The College Prowler™ Grade on

Parking: F

A high grade in this section indicates that parking is both available and affordable, and that parking enforcement isn't overly severe.

Transportation

The Lowdown On...
Transportation

Ways to Get Around:
On Campus:
By foot

Public Transportation:
MTA operates the subway and bus—http://www.mta.info or ask attendants at subway stations for maps and schedules

Taxi Cabs:
If you need to reserve a car for airport transport or another important event, call Carmel Car and Limousine Service—(212) 666-6666. Otherwise, walk into the street and raise your hand in the air for the next yellow cab that rolls by. New Yorker Tip: If the lights are on, they're for hire. If not, no dice. Also note that sometimes certain lights mean the cab is off-duty.

→

Best Ways to Get Around Town:

Subway

Bus

Cab

Ways to Get Out of Town:

Between Newark, LaGuardia, and JFK you can fly in and out of town on any airline you want.

Metro-North trains go to upstate New York and Connecticut. Amtrak services the northeast corridor and points west.

Airport:

The M60 bus leaves from Columbia's gates and will drop you at whatever terminal you need at LaGuardia for the regular bus fare.

JFK is accessible by the A train, approximately two hours away, cost $2.00. There's a shuttle from Grand Central station that costs $10 and a cab will run you about forty bucks.

The new AirTrain high speed train leaves Penn Station for Newark every half hour.

All Greyhound buses leave from Port Authority, at Times Square.

Travel Agents:

There's an STA Travel office in Lerner Hall, the student center.

Students Speak Out On...
Transportation

"The subway is your friend, and you will quickly learn how to maneuver and transfer like a pro. Cabs are also abundant and inexpensive if you are going with other people. There is also the trusty old bus. Any of the choices are quick, usually inexpensive, and pretty user-friendly."

Q "The subway and bus lines **take some getting used to**, especially for people who love the independence associate with having access to a car, but they are simple to use. Public transportation in New York is cheap and it takes you within a block or two of where you want to go at any time. The only problem is that Murphy's Law often comes into play when waiting for a subway. When you are running late, so is the train. When you have all the time in the world, the train is there to greet you. This makes planing meeting times a bit difficult. You need to give yourself a fifteen-minute time cushion to get anywhere because you never know if the trains will be there right when you need them. Cabs are a good alternative for those who hate to wait for the subway. If you have a few people with you, splitting a cab ride downtown is not a great expense."

Q "The **bus or a subway will take you wherever you need to go.** The greatest thing about it is that they run all night long too."

Q "The subways can take you anywhere you want to go in the whole city, and **the ratio of taxis to people is incredible.** I never have a problem getting a cab anywhere!"

Q "The subway is great, **it is so fast and you can get anywhere.** However I hate the ride up on the 9 train which is always too crowded when coming uptown especially in the morning. I feel like a sardine who is put in a can that is already overflowing. The bus is ridiculously slow, it has a rate about 1/2 hour for every 3 blocks. I remember once I was on the bus and these men were onversing in Spanish and saying "that's where we are? We have not really moved at all in about an hour?" I thought to myself that I could have walked faster than the bus and already have gotten home and had my dinner."

Q "The subway system is **very convenient and simple to use**. It runs for 24 hours a day. Within a few days, you will be a master. Cabs are also all around at all times. New York City takes the prize in this category, my friend!"

Q "There are **subway and bus stops just outside the Columbia gates.**"

Q "NYC is **famous for its MTA transportation system.** One of the largest in the world. Once you know it, you can travel anywhere in the world without fear."

Q "New York couldn't function without public transportation. **Fare changes and construction are annoying.**"

Q "There are **trains that will even take you all over New England** if you want to get away!"

Q "There is a **subway stop right on campus** as well as a few bus stops. You will be using them both constantly."

Q "Public transportation in New York is the best in the country. **I love it. It's safe, everyone uses it**, and it's really efficient. The City does a great job with this."

The College Prowler Take On...
Transportation

Just outside of Columbia's gates are a subway station and a bus stop. You can get anywhere in New York by using public transportation and it's open 24 hours a day, 7 days a week. The subway is cheap and relatively convenient. Although it takes some students awhile to get a hang of it, they all agree that it is easy to get around by public transportation. The bus is also a favorite because it allows people to actually see where they are going. Some students just hate the subway and they choose to take a cab. A cab is worth the extra expense if you hate lines and want to get somewhere faster or if you are suffering from a little bit of car envy.

Unlike many schools, Columbia students rely on public transportation and their feet to get around the city. There is nowhere a Columbia student cannot get to by using the MTA system. You can really get anywhere in the city with a Metrocard, as long as you have time, a map, and a couple of bucks—Metrocards are available at any subway station, just two dollars for one trip on the subway or bus.

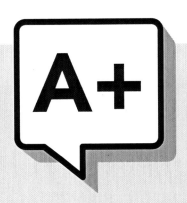

The College Prowler™ Grade on

Transportation: A+

A high grade for Transportation indicates that campus buses, public buses, cabs, and rental cars are readily-available and affordable. Other determining factors include proximity to an airport and the necessity of transportation.

Weather

The Lowdown On...
Weather

Average Temperature:
Fall: 58°F
Winter: 32°F
Spring: 53 °F
Summer: 77°F

Average Precipitation:
Fall: 3.14 in.
Winter: 3.74 in.
Spring: 4.44 in.
Summer: 4.22 in

Students Speak Out On...
Weather

> **"Summers in New York are magnificent. Too bad winters are so long. Leave your wardrobe at home and update it with NY fabulousness!"**

Q "New York can be freezing in the winter and it's hot and humid in the summer. **Layering clothing is essential to winter survival** because you are constantly moving in and out of heated classrooms to cold halls. Bring a coat that is waterproof and easy to put on and take off. Hats, scarves and gloves are a must too."

Q "Summer in this city is gross. There is **a layer of slime that coats everyone's skin** from late spring until fall arrives. Bring clothing that breathes because air conditioning is a luxury that most people choose not to possess. Bring baby powder. Lots of it."

Q "**Bring an umbrella**, or two."

Q "Columbia experiences **all four seasons!**"

Q "Mild in spring, **cold cold cold the rest of the time.** Be prepared for very cold weather, though it isn't consistently bad."

Q "New York gets **very cold, windy and wet in the wintertime.** In the summer, however, the weather is hot, humid and sticky. You're going to want to break out your coats and sweaters and you're going to want to bring not only some of your lightweight summer gear but an air conditioner as well."

Q "Go to Kenneth Cole. **Wear black.**"

Q "I'm from California, so **I miss the sunshine every now and then**, but New York is absolutely beautiful. The past winter was mild, so I can't say I've been in below-zero weather. Springtime and fall are gorgeous. I love to go for runs in Riverside Park."

Q "Okay, New York City **sucks in the winter and summer,** but fortunately, it's been really mild this past year. Winter sucks because it's not only cold but also windy; it's really humid in the summer. Every other season is comfortable."

Q "It's weird. I despise the cold. **When I left school in May, it was in the 40s and rainy.**"

Q "**Extreme weather is the name of the game.** It will be very hot and muggy when you move in, but once fall kicks in, it's time to break out the winter coats. January and February are white winters."

Q "New York weather is **pretty unpredictable.** It tends to stay pretty cool for the most part, but it didn't snow as much as I would've liked. I find cooler weather incredibly wonderful."

Q "The weather here is the typical four seasons—**cold and snowy in the winter**, hot and humid in the summer. But New York also has some unpredictable weather. This spring was pretty cold. I remember it was 80 degrees one week and then the week after, it was 40 or 50 degrees. It's kind of weird sometimes. During the winter, you'll just get sick of the cold—that's when everyone falls into some sort of slump."

Q "The weather is usually **pretty decent.** In the winter, we usually get some snow, but the walkways and roads are always cleared almost immediately. I've never spent the summer in the city, but it can get quite humid during the first and last months of school."

Q "It's New York, and **it's supposed to be cold**, but this year, it was only cold for a little bit. I guess the global warming is making traditionally cold regions warmer."

Q "This year, the weather was **unbelievably mild**—not hot not cold—for most of the year! The beginning and end of the school year can get hot. Usually, winters in New York are pretty cold but really fun—the cold weather, the snow, and the lights and decorations ... it's a great time to be around."

The College Prowler Take On...
Weather

New York has all four seasons, although spring and fall seem rather short. The humidity is a problem for many in the summer, and the snow, ice and wind are tough to take in the winter. Students seem to either love or hate the weather in New York. It is a source of both pleasure and pain and some find the inconsistency to be a curse.

New York is often wet, regardless of the season. Surprise thunderstorms are known to pop up and you end up looking like a drowned rat. Bring lots of layers because you'll wear everything you own on a snowy winter's day and you'll want to strip down to your skivvies in the summer to beat the heat. Expect weather as diverse as the people in New York.

B-

The College Prowler™ Grade on

Weather: B-

A high Weather grade designates that temperatures are mild and rarely reach extremes, that the campus tends to be sunny rather than rainy, and that weather is fairly consistent rather than unpredictable.

Report Card Summary

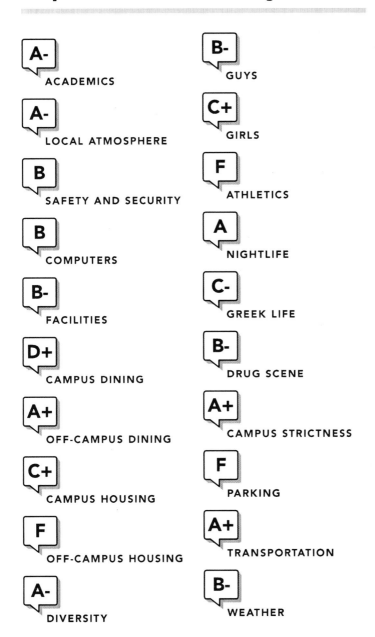

A- ACADEMICS

A- LOCAL ATMOSPHERE

B SAFETY AND SECURITY

B COMPUTERS

B- FACILITIES

D+ CAMPUS DINING

A+ OFF-CAMPUS DINING

C+ CAMPUS HOUSING

F OFF-CAMPUS HOUSING

A- DIVERSITY

B- GUYS

C+ GIRLS

F ATHLETICS

A NIGHTLIFE

C- GREEK LIFE

B- DRUG SCENE

A+ CAMPUS STRICTNESS

F PARKING

A+ TRANSPORTATION

B- WEATHER

Overall Experience

Students Speak Out On...
Overall Experience

"It's still exciting just to walk through the gates knowing that I am part of such a grand institution. I have enjoyed almost everything about attending this school and there is nowhere else I would rather be."

Q "I love Columbia. Think **I'll force my kids to go** (once they are born, of course)!"

Q **"I am really happy with Columbia.** I love pretty much everything about it! I don't think that I could be happier anywhere else. The school is awesome, classes are hard but not impossible, and the core is a pain but a blessing in disguise—I have learned so much because of it, and sometimes, it can actually be fun."

Q "Sometimes I wish I was somewhere more relaxed, and warmer, but right now **I wouldn't trade anything for the city.** It takes effort, the school doesn't really help you much, so you have to do a lot on your own. That can be a good thing if you've got the guts."

Q "All I can say is that **New York City is a great place.** The bars, clubs, and people are real cool. They call it 'The City That Never Sleeps.' Well, that's definitely true."

Q "If I had known, I probably would have gone to Smith or Vassar instead. The academics are really good but in many ways **you do not learn enough for the amount of money that you are paying**. I wish I had more caring counselors and people to tailor my program for me. I was one of those people who slipped through the cracks and had to struggle in the advanced classes because I never got my basics down-pat. All in all, I learned a lot and had a good experience but I probably would have decided differently had I known what I know now."

Q "Overall, **I'd have to say my experience at Columbia was very good.** Especially in my first and last years there, I feel like I got to experience a lot of New York. I don't know of any other place where the same amount of social opportunities is available. I am big on nightlife and found both the local bar scene as well as the bar and club scene in the entire city to be unparallel with any other city I've been to. The one thing that you should make sure about when coming to Columbia is whether you want a school where people will hold your hand or one where you're on your own. There is very little hand-holding at Columbia, and you are more or less on your own. Your support system is really primarily the friends you make. I think that the school is changing advising systems next year so that each student will be assigned a particular class dean as an advisor, so that may be helpful. However, if you are independent and want to take advantage of all of the opportunities that New York has to offer, Columbia is definitely the right place for you. It's extremely well-recognized in terms of getting jobs."

Q "Columbia has **been like a dream to me.** There's no place I would rather be. It truly is the consummate urban campus and I have really grown to love the city."

Q "What gives me continued satisfaction is knowing **I picked the perfect place for me!**"

Q "All I can tell you is that **it is an Ivy League school and a real honor to get into.** It has an outstanding academic record. I graduated at the top of my class and had my choices of graduate schools; I chose Columbia."

Q "I love Columbia. **I feel like I've made the right choice.** There is red tape to get through and a sometimes-distant administration, but there are tons of ways to get involved, and the people you will meet are incredible."

Q "Columbia is great**. It's very bureaucratic, and the faculty is not very responsive**, but there are so many opportunities in New York. It can be a bit overwhelming, but is really amazing nonetheless."

Q "I love Columbia. **I can't believe I've been here for two years**, and I wish I could stay here for longer. It's an excellent school in an excellent city. They have these 'Urban NY' events, in which you get free tickets to Broadway shows and theater and stuff; it's just cool."

Q "For me, **Columbia was the perfect choice**, as I wanted to get away from home and live life in the real world. New York City is the place to be."

Q "I applied to Columbia early decision without ever having visited the campus. **I absolutely fell in love with it** when I arrived. It's in the city, but the campus is absolutely gorgeous. I love the school, the people, and the general atmosphere. I don't regret that I came here at all. There's so much to be said for New York and Columbia. The opportunities are endless."

Q "Having always lived in New York City, **I would definitely recommend that people come and experience it** as well. It is a great city, but not for everyone. If you are not accepting of diversity and are close-minded, it is not the place for you."

Q "The most important thing is that **if you want to live in New York, come to Columbia.** If you don't want to live in New York, don't come to Columbia. It's pretty simple."

Q "It was **the most amazing experience of my academic life**, both as an undergrad and graduate student. As part of the Ivy League, this makes you special and separates you from the rest of the pack."

Q "Overall, **I love attending Columbia.** My only regret is that there is not a big athletic or Greek scene."

Q **"I am done and have no regrets.** I met some awesome people who I will never forget, and I plan on keeping in touch with dozens of them. One of the great things about Columbia is that it is in New York City; many students end up staying here after graduating."

Q "Columbia is a good school. **My only complaint is that they don't really care about their students**, and yet they wonder why we had three kids throw themselves out windows or off buildings this year. It's a really tough and stressful school, but it's challenging, and it's what I want in a college experience. Socially, I suppose I didn't get to experience as much as I should have, but there are really some great people there that I've had the good fortune to meet and befriend. As stressed as the school made me last year, I know that, academically and intellectually, it is where I belong. I had some rough experiences but, otherwise, my experience has been pretty challenging but very good and one that I will never regret."

Q "Lots of people at Columbia either **convince themselves they love it** or wish they were somewhere else."

Q "If you are interested in being around a diverse student body, a strong education program, and the benefits of living in New York City, **I would recommend Columbia**. It is a very safe campus, and there are security stations everywhere. It is not a dangerous neighborhood; there are tons of students living around the area. The campus food is pretty good, but not gourmet. The drinking spots are endless, and the campus spots are okay, but the focus at Columbia is not partying, it's studying and making connections in New York City."

The College Prowler Take On...
Overall Experience

Most students absolutely love Columbia. They discovered the
school that filled their academic, social and professional needs.
Since Columbia is so selective, most people who attend are
thrilled to be here and would never wish to be anywhere else.

Columbia has the potential to give any student what they are
looking for—be it prestige, socialization, culture, and a degree
from one of the finest schools in the world. The city is not
for the weak-hearted. Those who need hand-holding may not
find that kind of support here, but then again, they might, if
they look in the right place. It takes time to find and access
the things you want and need (and often students at Columbia discover fulfillment in things they never thought they'd
like before like exploring the city late at night or finding joy
in Medieval Italian Literature), but if you're willing to work a
little bit and leave a little up to chance, you may get more out
of college than most of your high school friends who went to
smaller, less diverse schools with fewer opportunities. Sure,
there are some disappointments, but on the whole there is no
place like Columbia in the City of New York—a place where you
can not only get an Ivy League education but also enjoy everything that the most exciting city in the world has to offer.

The Inside Scoop

The Lowdown On...
The Inside Scoop

Columbia Slang

Know the slang, know the school. The following is a list of things you really need to know before coming to Columbia. The more of these words you know, the better off you'll be.

Lit Hum

"Literature Humanities" in the bulletin, everybody, even the freshmen enjoying this required first-year literature call the course Lit Hum.

CC

"Contemporary Civilizations," the required political and philosophical thought course for second-year students.

Courseworks at Columbia

An online chat room where the faculty posts syllabi and students can learn about assignments and grades. www.columbia.edu and then double click on Courses.

CULPA

This is the online resource for students wishing to glean what others think about professors at Columbia. Just type CUPLA in the Columbia search engine and you will find stuff about nearly every professor.

L&R

Your freshman composition course, aka Logic & Rhetoric.

The 'Stend

an affectionate, if dorky, slang term for the bar and restaurant, The West End.

Jay

John Jay is the dormitory and its dining hall has the same name. But to all, it's Jay and if you ask your Carman suitemates if they want to go to Jay at 6 p.m., they'll know you mean to have dinner, not just kick it in the lounge.

"The class is taught by a graduate student."

To your mother, this means that a T.A. or teaching assistant is teaching your class. To you, it means that someone who's quite close to your age will be responsible for instructing you and grading you.

Lutomski

Rob Lutomski is in fact a real person, and is even spotted frequently on campus. But most CU students know him as the man who controls their fate—their housing fate that is. We usually only see him once a year, during the ten minutes that we select our room. But wielding that red pen, he might as well be God.

Hammie's

Hamilton Deli on 116th Street and Amsterdam, producers of all kinds of hangover-curing hoagies. They deliver.

Star-sixing

The ROLM phone system is the cornerstone of Columbia culture. Star-six is the pivotal ROLM command. It stops the message you're listening to in the middle and then deletes it. Comes in handy when you receive approximately one broadcast message a night from the university.

Things I Wish I Knew
Before Coming to Columbia

- That the Core curriculum took as much time as it did and that it was worth every second. You will spend two years fulfilling your core requirements, but you'll be a better person when you're done. And a lot smarter.

- That Columbia is an intimidating place. A lot of kids have a hard time settling in at Columbia, becaues there's a feeling that everyone else knows what's going on when you don't. It's a lie—nobody knows what's going on at Columbia, everyone just makes it up.

- That you can really do whatever you want at Columbia and New York and as long as it's not illegal, you can probably get away with it.

- That New York is absolutely the most expensive place you could ever go to college and fun has a pretty big price tag. Flip some extra burgers before the summer ends; you'll need some cash lying around. (And though I don't recommend bank robbery, it could be helpful).

- While Columbia is good about accepting up to 60 transferable credits, the administration is very picky about what classes live up to "Columbia Standards." Double check with advisers to make sure that your transferable math and humanities classes fill Columbia's specific needs. You don't want to find out at the last minute that your Renaissance Art class that you took at another college is not considered to be good enough for this one.

- While Columbia is a safe place to live and go to school, it is important to let people know where you will be. Let a friend know if you will be staying out all night. While this may sound silly, it's good to know that someone will know if you are missing.

- Financial aid is readily available for those who need it. While an application process is required, it's rather simple to get some extra help from the oft-generous Columbia coffers.

- Although there are two no-charge Citibank ATMs in Lerner Hall, the lines are excruciatingly long on Thursday afternoons and Friday nights. Get your cash ahead of time or be prepared for a long wait.

Things I Wish I Knew (continued)

- The Media Center in Butler Library is packed during midterms and finals. Reserve course materials are easy to come by at any other time of the semester, but not at finals time. If you need to watch a film for a class or read a book on reserve, make sure you give yourself enough time to access necessary materials. Waiting until the last minute is never a good idea during crunch time, because procrastination is not an original idea.

Tips to Succeed at Columbia

- Don't be afraid to march into any administrator's office if you need help or guidance. Nobody will ask you if you're doing OK, but they will stand up and listen if you shout that you need help, whether it's with academics, your personal health, your roommate or your mother.

- Explore. The more adventurous you are at Columbia and New York, the more little and big gems you'll discover. The city contains lots of thrills and also charms, waiting to be stumbled upon by you.

- Study what you want and how you want. Columbia isn't really a grade-grubbing place, especially compared to Harvard or Princeton, but you may sense occassionally that everyone around you is stressing out constantly and studying all the time. The less you pressure yourself, the better you'll do and all Columbia kids will say that they are in the library working on their thesis or studying for finals because they like the subject they're working on, not just because they have to.

- Be who you are and trust that you will find people that you like and who like you. It won't happen overnight, but it will happen—there are all kinds at Columbia.

- Do not wait until the last semester of your senior year to take all of your difficult classes. While some participate in the graduation events with one class left to go, there is something far more fulfilling about walking with your class knowing that you are a free (well, probably not debt-free) citizen.

- Utilize the campus tutorial services before you actually need them.

Columbia Urban Legends

- Probably the biggest rumor is that it's in Harlem and it's dangerous. Columbia does border on Harlem, but it's in a separate neighborhood. Furthermore, Harlem is a safe neighborhood—there are a lot of families there and now Columbia students who've spilt over into slightly less expensive housing. Acting like a snotty Ivy League kid won't make you friends in any neighborhood, but common courtesy and human respect will guarantee your safety.

- The Alma Mater statue in front of Low Library doubles as a mythical matchmaker. It is rumored that the first boy to spot the owl hidden within her robes will be valedictorian and the girl who finds it will marry him. Of course, this is an antiquated and sexist tradition, especially since many valedictorians are women, but members of the lonley-hearts club seek out this elusive owl anyway.

- Barnard to bed, Columbia to wed. You'll have to come test-drive that one yourself.

School Spirit

Students are often very proud of going to such a well-respected university, but you won't hear anyone screaming "Go Fighting Lions" on game day. It's an intellectual spirit, not necessarily an athletic one.

Traditions

On midnight, the night before finals begin, you can hear Columbia students lean out their windows and scream at the top of their lungs. To some it's a stress reliever, to others an unpleasant sleep disturbance.

Finding a Job or Internship

The Lowdown On...
Finding a Job or Internship

The Career Center at Columbia has a lot of meetings and workshops, but most importantly, they have a comprehensive Web site of job listings. Employers looking for smart kids usually list on Columbia's Web site, which usually has 20 new listings during off-peak hiring moments, and up to a hundred if it's internship season (which starts in February and lasts clear on through April). You can have someone critique your resume at drop-in hours or attend many of the job fairs they arrange in Lerner Hall. Columbia is a great professional choice, even for undergrads, because you have fascinating work opportunities available to you in the big city. The Career Center definitely helps you take advantage of them.

Advice

The Career Services Web site always has good job listings, but that's only half the battle. Don't expect the fact that you go to Columbia to get you a job. You have to look professional and act professional (a lot of New York employers can be wary of snobby Ivy Leaguers, so watch that it doesn't work against you). Take advantage of interviewing workshops at CU if you're not so comfortable in interview situations.

Career Center Resources & Services:

You can get interview advice, cover letter and resume help, counseling about your future careers and see career counselors for any other concerns you may have. Check out www.cce.columbia.edu for the full lowdown on career services.

The Lowdown On...
Alumni

Website:
http://www.columbia.edu/cu/
alumni

Office:
Office of University Development and Alumni Relations
475 Riverside Drive, MC 7720
New York, NY 10115
(212) 870-3100

Services Available

The Alumni office maintains the alumni network, eCommunity, and solicits donations

Major Alumni Events

The Alumni office maintains the alumni network, eCommunity, and solicits donations

Alumni Publications

Columbia Magazine comes out four times a year and is sent to Columbia alumni all over the world.

Did You Know?

Lots of famous people go to and have gone to Columbia. Alexander Hamilton went to Columbia, but he never graduated. On the other hand, Julia Stiles, Joseph Gordon Levitt, Anna Paquin and Rider Strong are all pursuing undergraduate degrees at Columbia. Unfortunately though, they don't live in beautiful apartments or have glamourous lives—Julia Stiles ate in the freshman dining hall with her buddies during her freshman year and Anna Paquin is often seen at The West End drinking draft beer. So much for stardom.

Student Organizations

A complete list of student organizations can be found at http://www.columbia.edu/cu/groups.html

- Accion Boricua
- American Institute of Aeronautics and Astronautics
- American Institute of Chemical Engineers
- American Society of Civil Engineers (ASCE)
- American Society of Mechanical Engineers (ASME)
- Anime Club
- Armenian Club
- Asian American Alliance
- Asian American Society of Engineers (AASE)
- Asian Journal
- Asian Pacific American Awareness Month (APAAM)
- Association for Computing Machinery (ACM)
- Bach Society
- Ballroom Dance Society
- Biological Society
- Black Students Organization (BSO)
- The Blue and White
- The Blue Key Society
- Chandler Society for Undergraduate Chemistry
- Chess Club
- Chicano Caucus
- Chinese Students Club
- Clefhangers (a capella group)
- Club Bangla
- Club Zamana
- College Bowl

- Columbia Barnard Economics Society
- Columbia College Class of 1999
- Columbia Concerts
- Columbia East Asian Review
- Columbia Music Presents
- Columbia Musical Theatre Society
- Columbia Orchestra for Asian Music
- Columbia Organization of Rising Enterpreneurs (CORE)
- Columbia Review
- Columbia Sign Language Club (CU Sign)
- Columbia Television (CTV)
- Columbia University Emergency Medical Service (CAVA)
- Columbia University Film Productions (CUFP)
- Columbia University Glee Club
- Columbia University Gospel Choir
- Columbia University Opera Ensemble
- Columbia University Performing Arts League (CUPAL)
- Columbia University Wind Ensemble
- Conversio Virium (CV)
- Culinary Society
- Elementary Hip-Hop

- Federalist Paper (newspaper)
- Ferris Reel Film Society
- Games Club
- Grupo Quisqueyano (GQ)
- Haitian Students Association
- Hellas
- Helvidius
- Institute of Electrical and Electronic Engineers (IEEE)
- Institute of Industrial Engineers(IIE)
- Japan Club
- Jester of Columbia
- King's Crown Shakespeare Troupe
- Kingsmen (a capella group)
- Korean Students Association (KSA)
- Latino Heritage Month
- Liga Filipina
- Metrotones
- Mock Trial Team
- Model Congress
- Model United Nations
- MUSEO
- Museum Club
- National Society of Black Engineers
- Nightline--Telephone Peer Counseling
- Notes and Keys
- Orchesis (A Dance Group)
- Organization of Pakistani Students (OPS)

- Parlimentary Debate Team
- Philolexian Society
- Policy Debate Team
- Political Science Students Association (PSSA)
- Prangstgrup
- Queer Alliance
- Queers of Color
- Raw Elementz
- Romanian Society
- Russian International Association of Columbia
- Science Fiction Society
- Singapore Students Association
- Six Milks (improvisational comedy troupe)
- Societa Italiana
- Society of Automotive Engineering (SAE)
- Society of Hispanic Professional Engineers (SHPE)
- Society of Women Engineers (SWE)
- Sounds of China
- Spectrum Journal
- Student Organization of Latinos (SOL)
- Students Promoting Empowerment and Knowledge (SPEaK)
- Taiwanese American Students Association (TASA)
- Thai Student Association
- Turath
- Two Left Feet (comedy improv)
- Ukrainian Student Society
- United Students of Color Council
- Uptown Vocal (a capella group)
- Varsity Show
- Vietnamese Student Association
- WKCR-FM New York Radio
- African Students Association
- AHIMSA
- American Civil Liberties Union (ACLU)
- Amnesty International
- ASHA for Education
- Asian Baptist Student Koinonia (ABSK)
- Augustine Club
- Baha'i Club of Columbia University
- Baptist Campus Ministry
- Black Church at Columbia
- Campus Crusade for Christ (CCC)
- Cantonese Christian Fellowship
- Catholic Campus Ministry
- Columbia Adaptive Sports Organization
- Columbia Buddhist Meditation Group
- Columbia Chinese Bible Study Group
- Columbia College Conservative Club

- Columbia College Democrats
- Columbia College Libertarians
- Columbia College Republicans
- Columbia Global Justice
- Columbia Iranian Students Association
- Columbia Men Against Violence
- Columbia Political Union
- Columbia Standard
- Columbia Student Solidarity Network (CSSN)
- Columbia University Chinese Students & Scholars Association (CUCSSA)
- Columbia University College Democrats
- Falun Dafa
- Hindu Students Organization (Santana Dharma Sanga)
- Hong Kong Students and Scholars Society
- Indian Progressive Study Group
- Interfaith Library
- International Church
- Intervarsity Christian Fellowship
- Isma'ili Students Association
- Japan Karate Association
- Jubilation! (a capella group)
- Korea Campus Crusade for Christ (KCCC)
- Latter-Day Saints Student Association
- Lesbian, Bisexual and Gay Coalition
- Libertarians
- Muslim Students Association
- Native American Council
- Orthodox Christian Fellowship
- People For Peace
- Postcrypt Art Gallery
- Postcrypt Coffeehouse
- Roots and Culture
- Sikhs Society
- Standard
- Students for Choice
- Students for Economic and Environmental Justice
- Students for Sensible Drug Policy (SSDP@CU)
- Students United for Victory
- Take Back the Night
- Tibetan Studies Society/Students for a Free Tibet
- Toward Reconciliation
- Turkish Students Association
- University Bible Fellowship
- Advocacy Coalition
- Barnard-Columbia Earth Coalition
- Columbia/Barnard Hillel
- Community Impact
- G.E.D./Reality House
- Peace Games

The Best & The Worst

The Ten BEST Things About Columbia:

1	The Core Curriculum
2	New York City
3	Diversity of student body and opinion
4	Access to smart professors and curious peers
5	Access to culture, excitement, and danger
6	New York City
7	New York City
8	New York City
9	New York City
10	New York City

The Ten WORST Things About Columbia:

1 Its sometimes sluggish bureaucracy

2 Cost of education and cost of living

3 The eternal dilemma—studying or doing something cool and interesting in NYC

4 Cramped housing

5 The time it takes to settle into your niche

6 Lerner Hall—the ugliest, most useful building on campus

7 The fact that it's not as well-located as NYU

8 Never being able to get a seat in Butler library

9 The very slow and disorganized mail system and package rooms

10 Coming home to your high school friends who haven't had nearly as interesting a year as you have

Visiting Columbia

The Lowdown On...
Visiting Columbia

Hotel Information

The following hotels offer discounts when you mention Columbia University while making a reservation. Keep in mind that hotels can be quite pricey in Manhattan, so consulting a discount hotel Web site may also be advisable. Rates below are based on double occupany during peak season; they are subject to change.

Beekman Tower Hotel

3 Mitchell Place, 49th Street & 1st Avenue

(212) 355-7300
or (800) 637-8483

$180/night

Belvedere Hotel

319 West 48th Street, between 8th & 9th Avenues

(212) 345-7000
or (888) HOTEL-58

belvedere@newyorkhotel.com

$175/night

→

The Benjamin Hotel

125 East 50th Street,
Lexington Avenue
(212) 715-2500
or (800) 637-8483
$235/night

Eastgate Tower Hotel

222 East 39th Street, between
2nd and 3rd Avenues
(212) 687-8000
or (800) 637-8483
$150/night

Empire Hotel

44 West 63rd Street, between
Broadway and Columbus
Avenue
(212) 265-7400
or (888) 822-3555
reservations@empirehotel.com
$160/night

Hotel Beacon

2130 Broadway at 75th Street
(212) 787-1100 ext. 623
info@beaconhotel.com
$145/night

Hudson Hotel

356 West 58th Street, between
8th and 9th Avenues
(800) 444-4786
$185/night

Hotel Newton

2528 Broadway at 96th Street
(212) 678-6500
or (800) 643-5553
newton@newyorkhotel.com
$105/night

The Lucerne

79th Street and
Amsterdam Avenue
(212) 875-1000 ext. 80
or (800) 492-8122
Lucerne@newyorkhotel.com
$170/night

The Mayflower Hotel On the Park:

15 Central Park West at 61st
Street
(212-865-0600)
or (800) 223-4160
resinfo@mayflowerny.com
$180/night

Novotel

226 West 52nd Street,
between Broadway and 8th
Avenue
(212) 315-0100
or (800) NOVOTEL
H0753@accor-hotes.com
$219/night

On the Ave

2178 Broadway at 77th Street
(212) 362-1100
or (800) 497-6028
ontheave@stayinny.com
$165/night

The Travel Inn Hotel
515 West 42nd Street between
10th & 11th Avenues
(212) 695-7171
or (800) 869-4630
$125/night

W New York
541 Lexington Avenue
at 49th Street
(212) 685-1100
$269/night

**W New York
Times Square Hotel**
1567 Broadway at 47th Street
(212) 755-1200
$309/night

Take a Campus Virtual Tour
http://www.studentaffairs.columbia.edu/admissions/
virtualvisit/.

To Schedule a Group Information Session
Undergraduate information sessions and tours are offered
Monday through Friday. Information sessions begin at 10
am and 2 pm followed by tours at 11 am and 3 pm. An
information session and campus tour is also offered the
second Saturday of each month, beginning at 10 am. From
September 13 to November 22, 2003, tours and information
sessions will be offered every Saturday, beginning at 10 am.

Overnight Visits:
Overnight visits are available Monday through Thursday
night. The link below will give you registration information for
overnight visits. http://www.studentaffairs.columbia.edu/
admissions/events/overnight.php.

To Schedule an Interview:
Interviews are not required for admission and may be arranged
off-site with Columbia alumni. Contact the admissions office
for more information.

Directions to Campus

Driving from the North:

Take the New York Thruway (I-87) or the New England Thruway (I-95) south to the Cross Bronx Expressway (I-95) in the direction of the George Washington Bridge. Take the exit for the Henry Hudson Parkway south (the last exit before the bridge). Exit the Parkway at West 95th Street and Riverside Drive. Go north on Riverside Drive to 116th Street. Turn right and go two blocks to Broadway and the University's main gate. Please note that the main gate is not open to traffic.

Driving from the South or West:

Take the New Jersey Turnpike north or I-80 east to the George Washington Bridge. As you cross the bridge, take the exit for the Henry Hudson Parkway south. Exit the Parkway at West 95th Street and Riverside Drive and follow the directions. Go north on Riverside Drive to 116th Street. Turn right and go two blocks to Broadway and the University's main gate. Please note that the main gate is not open to traffic.

Words to Know

Academic Probation – A student can receive this if they fail to keep up with their school's academic minimums. Those who are unable to improve their grades after receiving this warning can possibly face dismissal.

Beer Pong / Beirut – A drinking game with numerous cups of beer arranged in a particular pattern on each side of a table. The goal is to get a ping pong ball into one of the opponent's cups by throwing the ball or hitting it with a paddle. If the ball lands in a cup, the opponent is required to drink the beer.

Bid – An invitation from a fraternity or sorority to pledge their specific house.

Blue-Light Phone – Brightly-colored phone posts with a blue light bulb on top. These phones exist for security purposes and are located at various outside locations around most campuses. If a student has an emergency or is feeling endangered, they can pick up one of these phones (free of charge) to connect with campus police or an escort service.

Campus Police – Policemen who are specifically assigned to a given institution. Campus police are not regular city officers; they are employed by the university in a full-time capacity.

Club Sports – A level of sports that falls somewhere between varsity and intramural. If a student is unable to commit to a varsity team but has a lot of passion for athletics, a club sport could be a better, less intense option. If a club sport still requires too much commitment, intramurals often involve no traveling and a lot less time.

Cocaine – An illegal drug. Also known as "coke" or "blow," cocaine often resembles a white crystalline or powdery substance. It is highly addictive and dangerous.

Common Application – An application that students can use to apply to multiple schools.

Course Registration – The time when a student selects what courses they would like for the upcoming quarter or semester. Prior to registration, it is best to have an idea of several back-up courses in case a particular class becomes full. If a course is full, a student can place themselves on the waitlist, although this still does not guarantee entry.

Division Athletics – Athletics range from Division I to Division III. Division IA is the most competitive, while Division III is considered to be the least competitive.

Dorm – Short for dormitory, a dorm is an on-campus housing facility. Dorms can provide a range of options from suite-style rooms to more communal options that include shared bathrooms. Most first-year students live in dorms. Some upperclassmen who wish to stay on campus also choose this option.

Early Action – A way to apply to a school and get an early acceptance response without a binding commitment. This is a system that is becoming less and less available.

Early Decision – An option that students should use only if they are positive that a place is their dream school. If a student applies to a school using the early decision option and is admitted, they are required and bound to attend that university. Admission rates are usually higher with early decision students because the school knows that a student is making them their first choice.

Ecstasy – An illegal drug. Also known as "E" or "X," ecstasy looks like a pill and most resembles an aspirin. Considered a party drug, ecstasy is very dangerous and can be deadly.

Ethernet – An extremely fast internet connection that is usually available in most university-owned residence halls. To use an Ethernet connection properly, a student will need a network card and cable for their computer.

Fake ID – A counterfeit identification card that contains false information. Most commonly, students get fake IDs and change their birthdates so that they appear to be older than 21 (of legal drinking age). Even though it is illegal, many college students have fake IDs in hopes of purchasing alcohol or getting into bars.

Frosh – Slang for "freshmen."

Hazing – Initiation rituals that must be completed for membership into some fraternities or sororities. Numerous universities have outlawed hazing due to its degrading or dangerous requirements.

Sports (IMs) – A popular, and usually free, student activity where students create teams and compete against other groups for fun. These sports vary in competitiveness and can include a range of activities—everything from billiards to water polo. IM sports are a great way to meet people with similar interests.

Keg – Officially called a half barrel, a keg contains roughly 200 12-ounce servings of beer and is often found at college parties.

LSD – An illegal drug. Also known as acid, this hallucinogenic drug most commonly resembles a tab of paper.

Marijuana – An illegal drug. Also known as weed or pot; besides alcohol, marijuana is one of the most commonly-found drugs on campuses across the country.

Major –The focal point of a student's college studies; a specific topic that is studied for a degree. Examples of majors include physics, English, history, computer science, economics, business, and music. Many students decide on a specific major before arriving on campus, while others are simply "undecided" and figure it out later. Those who are extremely interested in two areas can also choose to double major.

Meal Block – The equivalent of one meal. Students on a "meal plan" usually receive a fixed number of meals per week.

Each meal, or "block," can be redeemed at the school's dining facilities in place of cash. More often than not, if a student fails to use their weekly allotment of meal blocks, they will be forfeited.

Minor – An additional focal point in a student's education. Often serving as a compliment or addition to a student's main area of focus, a minor has fewer requirements and prerequisites to fulfill than a major. Minors are not required for graduation from most schools; however some students who want to further explore many different interests choose to have both a major and a minor.

Mushrooms – An illegal drug. Also known as "shrooms," this drug looks like regular mushrooms but are extremely hallucinogenic.

Off-Campus Housing – Housing from a particular landlord or rental group that is not affiliated with the university. Depending on the college, off-campus housing can range from extremely popular to non-existent. Those students who choose to live off campus are typically given more freedom, but they also have to deal with things such as possible subletting scenarios, furniture, and bills. In addition to these factors, rental prices and distance often affect a student's decision to move off campus.

Office Hours – Time that teachers set aside for students who have questions about the coursework. Office hours are a good place for students to go over any problems and to show interest in the subject material.

Pledging – The time after a student has gone through rush, received a bid, and has chosen a particular fraternity or sorority they would like to join. Pledging usually lasts anywhere from one to two semesters. Once the pledging period is complete and a particular student has done everything that is required to become a member, they are considered a brother or sister. If a fraternity or a sorority would decide to "haze" a group of students, these initiation rituals would take place during the pledging period.

Private Institution – A school that does not use taxpayers dollars to help subsidize education costs. Private schools typically cost more than public schools and are usually smaller.

Prof – Slang for "professor."

Public Institution – A school that uses taxpayers dollars to help subsidize education costs. Public schools are often a good value for in-state residents and tend to be larger than most private colleges.

Quarter System (sometimes referred to as the Trimester System) – A type of academic calendar system. In this setup, students take classes for three academic periods. The first quarter usually starts in late September or early October and concludes right before Christmas. The second quarter usually starts around early to mid–January and finishes up around March or April. The last quarter, or "third quarter," usually starts in late March or early April and finishes up in late May or Mid-June. The fourth quarter is summer. The major difference between the quarter system and semester system is that students take more courses but with less coverage.

RA (Resident Assistant) – A student leader who is assigned to a particular floor in a dormitory in order to help to the other students who live there. A RA's duties include ensuring student safety and providing guidance or assistance wherever possible.

Recitation – An extension of a specific course; a "review" session of sorts. Because some classes are so large, recitations offer a setting with fewer students where students can ask questions and get help from professors or TAs in a more personalized environment. As a result, it is common for most large lecture classes to be supplemented with recitations.

Rolling Admissions – A form of admissions. Most commonly found at public institutions, schools with this type of policy continue to accept students throughout the year until their class sizes are met. For example, some schools begin accepting students as early as December and will continue to do so until April or May.

Room and Board – This is typically the combined cost of a university-owned room and a meal plan.

Room Draw/Housing Lottery – A common way to pick on-campus room assignments for the following year. If a student decides to remain in university-owned housing, they are assigned a unique number that, along with seniority, is used to choose their new rooms for the next year.

Rush – The period in which students can meet the brothers and sisters of a particular chapter and find out if a given fraternity or sorority is right for them. Rushing a fraternity or a sorority is not a requirement at any school. The goal of rush is to give students who are serious about pledging a feel for what to expect.

Semester System – The most common type of academic calendar system at college campuses. This setup typically includes two semesters in a given school year. The "fall" semester starts around the end of August or early September and finishes right before winter vacation. The "spring" semester usually starts in mid-January and ends around late April or May.

Student Center/Rec Center/Student Union – A common area on campus that often contains study areas, recreation facilities, and eateries. This building is often a good place to meet up with fellow students and is most commonly used as a hangout. Depending on the school, the student center can have a huge role or a non-existent role in campus life.

Student ID – A university-issued photo ID that serves as a student's key to many different functions within an institution. Some schools require students to show these cards in order to get into dorms, libraries, cafeterias, and other facilities. In addition to storing meal plan information, in some cases, a student ID can actually work as a debit card and allow students to purchase things from bookstores or local shops.

Suite – A type of dorm room. Unlike other places that have communal bathrooms that are shared by the entire floor, a suite has a private bathroom. Suite-style dorm rooms can house anywhere from two to ten students.

TA (Teacher's Assistant) – An undergraduate or grad student who helps in some manner with a specific course. In some cases, a TA will teach a class, assist a professor, grade assignments, or conduct office hours.

Undergraduate – A student who is in the process of studying for their Bachelor (college) degree.

ABOUT THE AUTHOR:

Michelle L. Tompkins hails from Sacramento, California and is the youngest of four children. Prior to attending Columbia University, she worked as a disc jockey for a Santa Rosa radio station, two Sacramento Theatre Companies and founded a talent agency in Los Angeles. When academia beckoned, she attended American River College in Sacramento and for two years was the Editor-in-Chief of the college newspaper the Current. At Columbia, she has served the past three years as Editor-in-Chief of the Observer, the literary and features magazine for Columbia School of General Studies. She will receive her BA in Film and will continue to work on creative writing projects in New York City.

michelletompkins@collegeprowler.com

Notes

Notes

....

....

....

....

....

....

....

....

....

....

....

....

....

Notes

Notes

....

....

....

....

....

....

....

....

....

....

....

....

....

Notes

....

....

....

....

....

....

....

....

....

....

....

....

....

Notes

Notes

Notes

....

....

....

....

....

....

....

....

....

....

....

....

....

....

Notes

Need More Help?

Do you have more questions about this school? Can't find a certain statistic? College Prowler is here to help. We are the best source of college information on the planet. We have a network of thousands of students who can get the latest information on any school to you ASAP. E-mail us at *info@collegeprowler.com* with your college-related questions. It's like having an older sibling show you the ropes!

Email Us Your College-Related Questions!

Check out **www.collegeprowler.com** for more details. 1.800.290.2682

Notes

....

....

....

....

....

....

....

....

....

....

....

....

....

Tell Us What Life Is Really Like At Your School!

Have you ever wanted to let people know what your school is really like? Now's your chance to help millions of high school students choose the right school.

Let your voice be heard and win cash and prizes!

Check out **www.collegeprowler.com** for more info!

Notes

Notes

....

....

....

....

....

....

....

....

....

....

....

....

....

Pros and Cons

Still can't figure out if this is the right school for you?
You've already read through this in-depth guide; why not
list the pros and cons? It will really help with narrowing down
your decision and determining whether or not
this school is right for you.

Pros	Cons

Notes

Need Help Paying For School?

Apply for our Scholarship!

College Prowler awards thousands of dollars a year to students who compose the best essays. E-mail *scholarship@collegeprowler.com* for more information, or call 1.800.290.2682.

Apply now at **www.collegeprowler.com**

Notes

Notes

Do You Own A Website?

Would you like to be an affiliate of one of the fastest-growing companies in the publishing industry? Our web affiliates generate a significant income based on customers whom they refer to our website. Start making some cash now! Contact *sales@collegeprowler.com* for more information or call 1.800.290.2682

Apply now at **www.collegeprowler.com**

Notes

....

....

....

....

....

....

....

....

....

....

....

....

....

....

Notes

....

....

....

....

....

....

....

....

....

....

....

....

....

Write For Us!
Get Published! Voice Your Opinion.

Writing a College Prowler guidebook is both fun and rewarding; our open-ended format allows your own creativity free reign. Our writers have been featured in national newspapers and have seen their names in bookstores across the country. Now is your chance to break into the publishing industry with one of the country's fastest-growing publishers!

Apply now at **www.collegeprowler.com**

Contact *editor@collegeprowler.com* or call 1.800.290.2682 for more details.

Notes

....
....
....
....
....
....
....
....
....
....
....
....
....